SAINT
MARGARET MARY

BOOKS BY MARY FABYAN WINDEATT

A Series of Twenty Books
Stories of the Saints for Young People ages 10 to 100

THE CHILDREN OF FATIMA
And Our Lady's Message to the World

THE CURÉ OF ARS
The Story of St. John Vianney, Patron Saint of Parish Priests

THE LITTLE FLOWER
The Story of St. Therese of the Child Jesus

PATRON SAINT OF FIRST COMMUNICANTS
The Story of Blessed Imelda Lambertini

THE MIRACULOUS MEDAL
The Story of Our Lady's Appearances to St. Catherine Labouré

ST. LOUIS DE MONTFORT
The Story of Our Lady's Slave, St. Louis Mary Grignion De Montfort

SAINT THOMAS AQUINAS
The Story of "The Dumb Ox"

SAINT CATHERINE OF SIENA
The Story of the Girl Who Saw Saints in the Sky

SAINT HYACINTH OF POLAND
The Story of the Apostle of the North

SAINT MARTIN DE PORRES
The Story of the Little Doctor of Lima, Peru

SAINT ROSE OF LIMA
The Story of the First Canonized Saint of the Americas

PAULINE JARICOT
Foundress of the Living Rosary & The Society for the Propagation of the Faith

SAINT DOMINIC
Preacher of the Rosary and Founder of the Dominican Order

SAINT PAUL THE APOSTLE
The Story of the Apostle to the Gentiles

SAINT BENEDICT
The Story of the Father of the Western Monks

KING DAVID AND HIS SONGS
A Story of the Psalms

SAINT MARGARET MARY
And the Promises of the Sacred Heart of Jesus

SAINT JOHN MASIAS
Marvelous Dominican Gatekeeper of Lima, Peru

SAINT FRANCIS SOLANO
Wonder-Worker of the New World and Apostle of Argentina and Peru

BLESSED MARIE OF NEW FRANCE
The Story of the First Missionary Sisters in Canada

SAINT MARGARET MARY

AND THE PROMISES OF
THE SACRED HEART OF JESUS

By
Mary Fabyan Windeatt

Illustrated by
Paul A. Grout

TAN BOOKS AND PUBLISHERS, INC.
Rockford, Illinois 61105

Nihil Obstat: Joseph D. Brokhage, S.T.D.
                  Censor Librorum

Imprimatur: ✠ Paul C. Schulte, D.D.
                  Archbishop of Indianapolis
                  Feast of Saint Margaret Mary
                  October 17, 1953

Library of Congress Catalog Card No.: 90-71825

ISBN: 0-89555-415-1

Printed and bound in the United States of America.

TAN BOOKS AND PUBLISHERS, INC.
P. O. Box 424
Rockford, Illinois 61105

1994

To those
who make known and loved
The Sacred Heart of Jesus.

CONTENTS

PRAYER TO THE SACRED HEART

O Heart of Love, I put all my trust in Thee; for I fear all things from my own weakness, but I hope for all things from Thy goodness.

—Saint Margaret Mary Alacoque

An indulgence of 300 days. A plenary indulgence once a month under the usual conditions, if this invocation is repeated daily with devotion. (Pius X, Rescript in his own hand, May 30, 1908, exhib. June 3, 1908; S.P. Ap., March 10, 1935.)

ACKNOWLEDGMENTS

Grateful acknowledgment is due the Reverend Thomas H. Moore, S.J., Editor of *The Messenger of the Sacred Heart* and National Secretary of the Apostleship of Prayer, for his help and encouragement in preparing this little story of Saint Margaret Mary Alacoque. Also to the Reverend Adrian Fuerst, O.S.B., S.T.D., Head of the Department of Social Studies at St. Meinrad Major Seminary, St. Meinrad, Indiana, and to the Reverend Victor L. Goossens, Pastor of St. Mary's Church, Indianapolis, Indiana, for the loan of much valuable source material.

SAINT
MARGARET MARY

SAINT MARGARET MARY ALACOQUE
1647-1690
THE APOSTLE OF THE SACRED HEART

CHAPTER 1

A TROUBLED HOUSEHOLD

THE PLUMP, good-natured face of Father Anthony Alacoque wore a worried frown as he trudged through the fields from his parish church at Verosvres to the neighboring farm of Lhautecour. True, the crops were splendid in this year of Our Lord 1660, and he himself in excellent health. Parish finances were satisfactory, too. But things were far different at Lhautecour for his widowed sister-in-law, Madame Philiberte Alacoque, and her poor little invalid daughter Margaret.

"It's a shame the way my own sisters are treating those two," mumbled the priest, pausing for a moment to survey the fertile countryside. "A shame and a disgrace. Today I must give Benedicta and Catherine a good talking-to."

But even as he neared Lhautecour and started purposefully toward the smaller of the two stone farmhouses, a woman's shrill voice echoed angrily from the kitchen.

"Philiberte, you clumsy fool! You've broken another dish! What in heaven's name is the matter with you?"

There was a moment's silence, then a burst of uncontrolled sobbing.

1

"But I couldn't help it, Benedicta! Truly I couldn't..."

"That's a likely story! You'll go without your dinner for this, my fine lady. Mark my words. Now, clean up that mess at once, do you hear? At once!"

"But I don't feel well—"

"Listen, stupid, if you don't do what I say..."

There was another burst of tears. Then, after a moment: "All right, Benedicta, I'm sorry. I'll pick up the pieces. Only please don't be angry with me! It was all just an accident. Truly it was!"

Father Anthony sighed and shook his head. Poor Philiberte! Her lot in life had certainly changed for the worse since the death of her beloved Claude five years ago. Before that she had been undisputed mistress of Lhautecour, and Claude the best and most generous of husbands.

Too generous, reflected Father Anthony ruefully, picking his way past the bedraggled geese, chickens and ducks aimlessly scratching in the courtyard. Now if Claude had only been a bit more careful with his money, a bit more insistent that his law clients pay their bills and that the servants should not waste their time, Lhautecour would certainly never have gone to rack and ruin. Then sharp-tongued Benedicta Delaroche and her husband Toussaint would not have had to try to save the place from bankruptcy. Or ill-tempered Catherine either. As for Grandmother, Toussaint's crotchety old mother who had also come to live at the farm—

"Well, may the Will of God be done," murmured the priest, bracing himself for the ordeal that lay ahead. "Lord, give me the right words to say to my sisters—and to Philiberte, too."

There was good need for such a prayer. As Father

Anthony pushed open the kitchen door, a frail, black-clad matron of some thirty-eight years immediately abandoned the bits of crockery which she had been trying to sweep into a pile and rushed tearfully toward him.

"Oh, Father! Thank God you've come! I . . . I'm so miserable I could die!"

The priest managed a reassuring smile. "There, there, my dear, what's the trouble? Surely you and Benedicta haven't been quarreling again!"

Across the room Benedicta Delaroche, a gaunt woman of forty-two, drew herself up to her full height. "Quarreling!" she burst out. "Anthony, if you weren't a priest of God and my own brother, I'd send you packing this very minute. As it is, will you tell Philiberte to go upstairs at once? It's high time you and I had an understanding about some things."

"Yes, and I want a few words with you, too," put in a second querulous voice. "I may not have a husband, but surely I ought to have some rights around this wretched place."

Father Anthony turned. His youngest sister Catherine, shabbily dressed and looking far older than her forty years, had followed him in from outside and now was fixing him with a suspicious glance.

"Why, Catherine! I never heard you come in."

"Of course you didn't, Anthony. I never intended that you should. Now, if you'll just send Philiberte about her business . . ."

Madame Alacoque dabbed at her reddened eyes. "Father, I don't have to go, do I? There's *so* much I want to tell you! And Margaret will want to talk to you, too, and to have your blessing. Poor little lamb, she's dying by inches, Father, and not a soul to care for her but me . . ."

"OH, FATHER, I'M SO MISERABLE..."

"That's a lie, Philiberte, and you know it!" snapped Benedicta Delaroche. "Margaret has had the best of treatment ever since she took sick four years ago. And who's paid for her food and medicine all that time? Who's kept a roof over her head, and yours? Why, if it weren't for all the hard work my husband and I have put in here at Lhautecour. . ."

Catherine Alacoque's thin lips trembled. "Don't forget that I've worked hard, too, Benedicta. Up early every morning, rain or shine. Scrubbing, cleaning, cooking, mending. And for what, I ask you? Oh, when I think of all that might have been. . ."

Father Anthony squirmed. Poor Catherine! An unfortunate love affair several years ago had completely soured a disposition none too cheerful by nature. Now, unless he were careful, she would begin to recount the whole miserable story for the thousandth time.

"Philiberte, I do think you'd better leave us for a while," he said hastily.

"But Father—"

"It's all right, my dear. We'll have a good visit together later on. I give you my word."

"And Margaret?"

"I'll see her, too. Never fear."

Slowly Madame Alacoque turned toward the door. "Very well," she said heavily. "I'll go."

CHAPTER 2

A BIG PROMISE

THIRTEEN-YEAR-OLD Margaret Alacoque moved ever so slightly in her wide oaken bed and opened her eyes. What a wonderful dream! And so real! She had been back at boarding school in Charolles, running a race with Genevieve, Annette and a dozen others of her classmates.

"And I won! I was the first to reach the big oak tree at the end of the garden!" the child recalled. Then, as a spasm of pain clutched her heart, a tear rolled down the pale cheeks of the little invalid. It had been good while it lasted, that dream, but it was over now.

"Dear Lord, please help me!" she whispered. "Don't let Mother find me crying. . ."

Suddenly there was a tap at the door and a kindly-faced old servant woman peered cautiously inside.

"Miss Margaret! Are you awake, child?"

Some of the pain left the young girl's face at the sight of her visitor, and her dark eyes brightened. "Felice! Oh, yes! Do come in!"

"Well, just for a minute, pet. See? I've brought you some grapes. Now, you will try to eat every one of them, won't you?"

Margaret managed a slight smile. The grapes did look

6

delicious, and of course Felice must have gone to great trouble to find them. But it was so hard to eat when one was never hungry. . .

"I. . . I'll take one, Felice. And thank you so much for thinking of me. But you really shouldn't—"

"Tut, tut, child. I know what I'm doing. Come, now. Couldn't you sit up a bit? Here, let Felice fix the pillows."

Margaret gritted her teeth. For four years a bad case of rheumatic fever had made it agony for her to be moved. Now, despite her best efforts to suppress it, a groan escaped the little sufferer's lips as the old woman tried to raise her to a new position.

"Oh, Felice! I. . . I can't help it! I ache so much. . . and all over. . ."

Felice clucked sympathetically. "Of course you do, poor lamb, when you're nothing but skin and bones. Oh, if you could just eat a little more—"

"But I'm never hungry, Felice."

"Well, you must try to eat these grapes all the same, precious. Here, now. Try this one for old Felice."

Obediently Margaret began to sample the grapes, but she had managed to swallow only two of them when an impatient voice echoed from the courtyard below.

"Felice, you lazy creature! Where are you? Come here at once!"

Margaret's eyes clouded. "I guess Grandmother wants you, Felice. You'd better go."

The old woman nodded grimly. "Yes, pet. But I'll be back again. Never fear. And there mustn't be one grape left when I do come. Remember that."

When the door had shut behind her trusted friend, Margaret gave a deep sigh and lay wearily back upon her pillows. What a pity that Grandmother, Aunt Catherine and Aunt Benedicta should work so long and hard as to be constantly tired and fretful! Always impatient with everyone else in the household, especially old Felice! Actually, of course, there was no reason why they couldn't take things a little easier now and then. But they were conscientious women. The debt against Lhautecour had to be wiped out, they insisted. And this was no small matter, after all the years of mismanagement under that good-for-nothing relative, Claude Alacoque.

"Poor Papa never meant to cause us so much trouble," thought Margaret sadly. "But he was just too kind a man to make people pay him what they owed." Then, after a moment: "Dear Lord, if there was only something I could do to help! It's so hard to be sick like this, and a burden on everyone..."

But even as these thoughts crossed her mind, Margaret put them aside. Hadn't Father Anthony told her that very morning, after giving her his blessing, that God had some good reason for permitting her to be ill so long? Of course it was hard not to know what this was, but surely someday everything would be clear. The main thing now was to pray for the gift of faith.

"Dear Father Anthony, how kind he is to me!" thought Margaret. "I always feel so much better after a visit with him. That's why I had that good sleep a while ago, and the nice dream. Now, perhaps if I shut my eyes again and try to have a great love of God's Will..."

However, this was no time for sleeping, for in a moment the door to Margaret's room opened a second time and Madame Alacoque, wide-eyed and fearful, came hurrying toward her daughter's bedside.

"Child, what's the trouble? I came as soon as I heard you call. Is the pain bad again?"

Margaret's dark eyes widened. "I didn't call you, Mama. I'm all right. Truly I am!"

"But I was sure I heard your voice, dear. And I was *so* worried..."

"No, Mama. I was just going to try to sleep a little, if I could."

Madame Alacoque sat down on a low stool near the window and burst into tears. "Then it's my nerves again!" she sobbed. "I keep hearing things all the time. Oh, dear God, what's going to become of us?"

"But Mama—"

"I can't stand any more of this, child! I can't! I can't!"

For a moment Margaret did not speak. Then she forced a faint smile. Perhaps fifteen-year-old Chrysostom or nine-year-old James, those high-spirited brothers of hers who were living with their uncle at his rectory in Verosvres, had been up to some kind of mischief again.

"No, child, that's not it," sighed Madame Alacoque, reading her daughter's thoughts. "This time it's John and Philibert."

"John and Philibert! But Mama, they've always been happy with the Benedictine monks at Cluny! Why, they wrote and told you so again only last week."

Madame Alacoque twisted her hands nervously. "I know. Still, your aunts think the boys have stayed long enough at the Abbey school and should come home to help with the farm. And Grandmother thinks the same. Oh, when I remember how your poor father wanted all you children to have the best possible education, no matter how long it took or what it cost..."

"But Father Anthony's paying the bills for John and Philibert," protested Margaret. "Besides, John's nearly twenty and Philibert eighteen. They'll soon be finished with school."

Suddenly an expression of fresh concern crossed Madame Alacoque's worn face. "Child, I shouldn't be worrying you like this," she exclaimed remorsefully, rising from her stool and coming over to the bed. "Poor little lamb, you have enough troubles of your own." Then, as Margaret's anxious eyes met hers: "Look, dear, perhaps if we prayed very hard to Our Lady for a cure. . ."

"But we *have* prayed, Mama! Over and over again."

"I know. But we've never promised her anything in return for a cure, have we?"

"N-no—"

Very gently Madame Alacoque took Margaret's thin hand in hers. "Well, then, let's promise her something very special, child. And then pray as we've never prayed before."

Margaret hesitated. "All right, Mama. But what shall we promise?"

Tears flooded Madame Alacoque's eyes. "Child, I love you so much! It would just about kill me to have you leave home. But if Our Lady wants you for her own. . .well, we mustn't hold back. We must do what she wants, no matter what it costs."

"You mean—?"

"I mean that the Blessed Virgin *may* cure you, dear, if you promise to be one of her daughters in some convent."

A flush of excitement crept into Margaret's pale cheeks as she pondered the surprising suggestion. She, a nun? Strong and well and able to work for others? Perhaps at the Poor Clare monastery in Charolles where she had been so happy as a student until she had fallen ill? What a thought!

Oh, Mama, let's do it!" she cried impulsively. "Let's make the promise—and right away!"

CHAPTER 3

NEW HEALTH AND NEW TROUBLES

WITHIN JUST a few weeks everyone in the neighborhood was talking about the wonder which had taken place at Lhautecour. Young Margaret Alacoque was actually recovering from the illness which had kept her bedridden for more than four years! She was even able to manage the mile-long walk to Sunday Mass at the parish church in Verosvres!

"But the child still looks like a little ghost," observed Peter Michon, a neighboring farmer. "A breath of wind could surely blow her away."

Madame Michon shrugged her shoulders. "Well, it'll be different after a while," she said knowingly. "Fresh air, sunshine, a chance to enjoy herself with other girls her own age—ah, that will make a big difference, Peter. Just wait and see if Margaret Alacoque doesn't turn into one of the prettiest young women around here. Why, maybe our own Charles—"

Peter Michon chuckled good-naturedly. "Maybe," he said, his eyes twinkling. "Charles could certainly do a lot worse."

Of course Margaret was delighted to be up and around again, to walk at will through the fields about Lhautecour, to visit Chrysostom and James at Father

11

Anthony's rectory, to offer heartfelt prayers of thanksgiving in the little parish church. However, about the time of her fourteenth birthday, her freedom was abruptly curtailed.

"Henceforth, Margaret, you'll not leave the house without permission," Benedicta Delaroche announced one day. "You're not sick any more, you know, and it's high time you started to be useful around here."

Her sister Catherine nodded grimly. "Yes. And you can start by scrubbing the kitchen floor right now."

"And when that's done, you can wash the windows," added Grandmother tartly.

Margaret's face fell. It was a beautiful day, and she had planned to gather wildflowers for Our Lady's shrine at the parish church.

"I . . . I'll be glad to help," she said hesitantly. "But please, when I'm through . . ."

"When you're through, you'll get busy at the mending," said Benedicta quickly, pointing to a large clothes hamper in the corner of the kitchen. "A farm's no place for idle hands, young lady. Your mother had to find that out long ago and now it's high time you did the same."

Poor Margaret! She had never been accustomed to hard physical work, and soon she was ready to drop with exhaustion. In fact, Madame Alacoque was well-nigh desperate when she came upon her daughter scrubbing the floor, pale-faced and struggling for breath.

"Benedicta, you'll kill the child!" she told her sister-in-law frantically. "Don't you know that rheumatic fever left her with a weak heart?"

"Nonsense!" said Benedicta Delaroche brusquely. "A dose of honest work never hurt anyone, Philiberte. Besides, can't you see that Margaret's a terribly puny little thing? Only skin and bones? What she needs is regular exercise to build her up."

"But—"

"Silence! No one here intends to spoil your daughter as you've spoiled her. As long as the girl is up and around, she'll do her fair share of work like everyone else."

In vain Madame Alacoque wept and pleaded. Until her son John reached his twenty-third birthday (and that was still two years distant), Benedicta Delaroche, her husband Toussaint and Grandmother were legal managers of Lhautecour and their orders must be obeyed.

As the months passed, Margaret did her best not to complain. Someday things would be very different at Lhautecour. John would return from the Benedictine school at Cluny, reimburse Uncle Toussaint for all his labor about the farm and then assume full responsibility for the place himself. A little later Philibert would also come home to help.

"Then all our troubles will be over, Mama," she said consolingly. "We'll have this place to ourselves again, just like in the old days. Besides—"

"W-what, dear?"

"We shouldn't forget that Uncle Toussaint has really worked hard to build up the farm since Papa's death. And Grandmother, Aunt Benedicta and Aunt Catherine, too. We *must* be grateful to them, Mama. It's only fair."

"Fair!" burst out Madame Alacoque tearfully. "Why, those three women are tyrants! Most days they don't even give us enough to eat, let alone decent clothes to wear. Oh, when I think of how things used to be—"

"There, there, Mama, please don't cry!" put in Margaret hastily. "Everything's going to be all right. Really it is!"

"IT'S ALL RIGHT, MAMA..."

However, as the days passed, Margaret's own courage often wavered. Overworked and undernourished, she had all she could do to keep from giving way to despair. Then in the fall of 1662 Madame Alacoque fell gravely ill and the doctor announced that there was nothing he could do to help.

"Your mother has a bad case of erysipelas," he told Margaret. "She can't possibly live until Christmas."

The fifteen-year-old girl was desperate. Poor Mama! How dreadful that she would never see the happy day when John would return to be master of Lhautecour!

"Dear Lord, please work a miracle!" was her constant prayer. "I don't know how I could bear it. . .to be left here all alone. . .with no real family. . ."

But the days passed, and Madame Alacoque's condition grew steadily worse. An ugly abscess formed on one side of her face, so large and painful as to affect her sight. In vain Father Anthony stormed Heaven for the cure of his sister-in-law—or at least for some relief from her sufferings. The invalid showed not the slightest sign of improvement. To make matters worse, Benedicta Delaroche and her sister Catherine stubbornly refused to enter the sickroom. Erysipelas was catching, they insisted. It would be folly (and Grandmother agreed with them) to expose themselves to infection.

Margaret's heart sank. She knew nothing about nursing. And Mama was *so* sick! What ever was going to happen?

CHAPTER 4

HAPPINESS RETURNS TO
THE ALACOQUE HOME

FERVENT AND continued prayer can work marvels. On New Year's Day, 1663, when Margaret returned from Mass at the parish church, she found that her mother's condition had taken a sudden turn for the better. The dreadful abscess had burst, and this brought considerable relief from pain for the invalid. Then early in the New Year, John Alacoque arrived at Lhautecour to take over the management of the farm—his studies at the Benedictine Abbey of Cluny finally completed.

"Poor little sister, you've had a hard time of it," he declared. "But it's all over now, my dear. I'm the master of Lhautecour, and no one else."

Margaret's heart almost burst with happiness. How good to have this big brother home! To know that Grandmother, Aunt Benedicta and Aunt Catherine were planning to leave the farm at once, and that never again would she and Mama have to suffer at their hands! And for that matter, it would be no hardship to say good-bye to Uncle Toussaint either. While he had never actually been cruel to Mama or herself, and had done good work in building up the farm, he had never made the slightest effort to make things pleasant, or to sympathize in any trouble. Not even when Aunt Benedicta had grown impatient with old Felice and angrily dismissed her from service had he shown the slightest concern.

However, in the happy days following John's return, Margaret found that she was still not without anxiety. More than two years ago she had made a vow that, if cured of her illness, she would give herself to the Blessed Virgin's service as a religious in some convent. Well, now that she was almost sixteen—

"John, I don't think I ought to keep Our Lady waiting any longer," she announced one day. "It wouldn't be right."

John Alacoque hesitated. While he could see his young sister's point of view, it was hard to think of losing her to the cloister so soon after his return.

"My dear, couldn't you wait a bit longer?" he asked anxiously. "At least until Philibert's finished school?"

Margaret's face fell. This would mean depriving the Blessed Virgin of two whole years of service!

"But John! I don't really see how—"

"Now, now, there's no need to have scruples. You know Mama isn't entirely well yet. How could you possibly think of leaving her alone to do all the housework?"

"But I did promise Our Lady—"

"I know. And someday you'll keep your promise. But not just now, Margaret, when you're so badly needed at home. Why, what would happen if Mama took sick again? Who'd look after her if I had to be away on business?"

Reluctantly Margaret admitted the reason in her brother's arguments. "All right," she said finally. "I won't bother you any more about wanting to be a nun,

John—at least not until Philibert has finished school."

Needless to say, twenty-three-year-old John Alacoque was immensely relieved to hear Margaret's decision. In fact, he was bubbling over with relief. And he was even happier when Margaret agreed to help him entertain his friends and neighbors from time to time. It would do no harm to have a little fun at Lhautecour, he said. After all, the place had been terribly gloomy during the reign of Grandmother, the two aunts and Uncle Toussaint. Misers that they were, these four had never welcomed visitors. Well, now all this must be changed. Lhautecour must become the happy house it was in the days when Papa had been alive—a gathering place for young and old—with plenty of food, drink, dancing, singing and games, especially on big feast days.

Margaret entered into the new order of things with greater satisfaction than she had thought possible. Before her childhood illness she had always been extremely active. Now sixteen years of age, in perfect health, with a generous allowance from John to spend as she saw fit, she soon found herself one of the most popular girls in the neighborhood. Yet despite these happy circumstances, there were occasional worries.

"I just love to dance," she told Father Anthony one day. "But do you think I ought to do so much of it, Father? Especially when I'm going to enter the convent someday?"

The priest smiled at the worried young face lifted to his. What an attractive girl his niece was turning out to be! Rosy cheeks, shining brown hair, the hunted look entirely gone from the large dark eyes—

"Now, child, these family parties are quite innocent affairs," he said kindly. "You haven't the slightest need to worry about them." Then, as Margaret continued to look anxious: "After all, Mama approves, doesn't she?"

The girl's face brightened. "Oh, yes, Father! She just loves to hear John say we're going to have the neighbors in again. In fact, she often joins in the singing and dancing herself! And the games, too."

"Well, then, my dear, you may do the same with a clear conscience. Indeed, you can turn all these little pleasures into prayers by thanking the good Lord for sending them to you."

Margaret's dark eyes widened. "I can, Father?"

"Of course. After all, if we sanctify the sorrow God sends us by not questioning the reason for its coming, why can't we do the same with joy? Both are from Him, you know."

This suggestion of her priest-uncle brought Margaret considerable peace, and in the weeks that followed she entered wholeheartedly into the various gay doings her brother planned. However, from time to time her thoughts did turn to a bothersome problem. Just which convent was she going to enter when Philibert returned from school? Once it had seemed that she ought to go to the Poor Clare nuns in Charolles, where she had been so happy as a child in boarding school. But of late something kept telling her that she was not meant to be a daughter of Saint Francis of Assisi. Nor was she meant to join another well-known Order, the Ursulines, as a young cousin of hers was thinking of doing. No, she must serve Our Lady in some other religious house.

"Where is it, dearest Mother?" she often asked. "Where is it that you want me to go when I'm eighteen?"

CHAPTER 5

SORROWS AND HOPES

ALAS FOR Margaret's hopes and plans! Less than a year after his return to Lhautecour, John Alacoque suddenly fell ill and died. Then tragedy struck again when Philibert (who had taken over the farm) followed his brother to the grave. Madame Alacoque was beside herself with grief. Years ago she had lost two small daughters, Catherine and Gilberte. That blow had been hard to bear. The death of her husband had been a terrible shock, too. But now to lose two grown sons, just when she needed them most...

"It's a punishment for sin!" she sobbed hysterically. "First John, then Philibert! Oh, Margaret, what have we done to offend the good God that He should treat us so?"

Margaret, heartbroken though she was at the loss of her two brothers, nevertheless tried to speak consolingly of Divine Providence and to lighten her mother's grief in every way she could. All was not lost, she pointed out. The two younger boys, Chrysostom and James, now at school with the Benedictine monks at Cluny, were strong and healthy. Of course young James would never be able to take over the farm, since he was planning to be a priest, but there was no reason why Chrysostom couldn't help out.

"No, no, he can't leave school at eighteen!" protested Madame Alacoque tearfully. "Papa wanted all his sons to have a good education. . .and if Chrysostom should come home now. . .in the middle of everything. . .oh, what *are* we going to do?"

However, young Chrysostom had ideas of his own. There was really no need for him to keep on going to school, he said. Although he had planned to be a full-fledged lawyer like his father, he would be just as happy living on the land. And so, shortly after Philibert's death, he arrived home to take over the management of Lhautecour.

For more than a year all went well. Then Madame Alacoque began to suffer from severe headaches, which left her irritable and out-of-sorts. When Chrysostom announced that soon he hoped to marry Angelica Aumonier (a pretty young girl whom he had known since childhood), she took to her bed with what amounted to a nervous breakdown.

"No, no!" she sobbed. "Angelica's not nearly good enough for you! Besides, you're much too young to marry anyone. . ."

Twenty-year-old Chrysostom could scarcely believe his ears. "Too young!" he stormed to Margaret at the first opportunity when they found themselves alone. "What's the matter with Mama? Doesn't she know I'm a man now, not a little boy? Can't she see I've done a man-sized job in making a success of the farm? Besides, what's all this foolishness about Angelica's not being good enough for me?"

In spite of herself Margaret had to smile at the sight of her brother's indignant face. "There, now, please

"PLEASE DON'T BE ANGRY, CHRYSOSTOM."

don't be angry, Chrysostom. Mama's not feeling well these days, you know."

"Maybe not. But what's she got against Angelica? Why, that girl is the prettiest, the kindest, the most cheerful person in the world. And holy, too. She'll make a wonderful daughter-in-law."

"Of course she will. Just the same, I think that Mama's a bit afraid of her."

"Afraid of Angelica? What nonsense, Margaret! Why, I've already explained. . ."

"I know. Your Angelica is the prettiest, the kindest, the most cheerful girl in the world. But you're forgetting one thing, Chrysostom. Something very important."

"And what's that?"

"If you married Angelica, you'd want to bring her to live at Lhautecour."

"Naturally, if I have to run the place."

"Well, Mama can't help remembering how things were for her when Aunt Benedicta, Aunt Catherine and Grandmother were living here. They were in-laws, too, you know, and made life miserable for her."

"But Angelica's nothing like those three, Margaret! She's sweet and kind and lovable—"

"Of course she is. Just the same, there are problems when two mistresses share the same house. And Mama's afraid that you'd always side with Angelica if any little troubles should come up."

For a moment Chrysostom was silent. Then slowly the hurt and indignation faded from his eyes. Poor Mama! He had forgotten all those miserable years following Papa's death. . .

"I. . .I'm sorry," he muttered. "I guess I've been terribly selfish, Margaret. Do you suppose if I waited a bit. . .and prayed about things. . .that Mama would come to understand?"

Margaret nodded cheerfully. "Of course," she said. "After all, Mama loves you dearly, Chrysostom. And no matter how she acts now, she really wants you to be happy."

Chrysostom hesitated. "Well, I could only be happy with Angelica," he declared firmly. "Oh, Margaret, will you pray with me that all this trouble will be settled—soon?"

Margaret stretched out a hand affectionately. "Of course I will," she said sympathetically. "That's surely the very least I could do."

CHAPTER 6

MARGARET'S INNER STRUGGLES

THE PRAYERS of brother and sister were answered far sooner than either had dared to hope. In fact, it was just a few weeks later—on January 30, 1666—that Father Anthony officiated at the wedding of Chrysostom and Angelica in the parish church at Verosvres. And no one was in higher spirits for the occasion than Madame Alacoque. Indeed, it was not too long before she was trying to make arrangements for a second wedding in the family.

"I've just gained a daughter and now I want a son," she told Margaret one day. "How about it, my dear? At least three young men have already spoken to me about wanting to marry you. And they've spoken to Chrysostom, too."

Nineteen-year-old Margaret's eyes widened in dismay. "But Mama, you know I couldn't possibly marry anyone! Why, the vow I made to Our Lady. . ."

Madame Alacoque shrugged. "Oh, that! Child, why not forget about the vow? After all, at thirteen you were far too young to know what you were doing. And sickly, too. Besides, I never should have suggested such a thing without first discussing matters with Father Anthony. It was very rash and imprudent of me."

25

Margaret's heart sank. What a thought, that Mama did not consider that long-ago promise to the Blessed Virgin to be a binding one! That possibly even Father Anthony. . .

"Mama, please don't be angry, but I really *want* to go to the convent."

"Now Margaret—"

"I'm grown-up, Mama. And I've known for a long time that I could never be happy living in the world."

Suddenly tears filled Madame Alacoque's eyes, and she began to cry as though her heart would break. "Y-you don't love me!" she sobbed. "You want to leave me all alone in my old age. . ."

"No, no, Mama. That's not it at all. But the vow—I just couldn't break it. Then, the voices. . ."

"What voices?"

"The voices in my heart, Mama. I hear them almost every day. One seems to belong to Our Lord, the other to the Blessed Virgin. And they tell me it's wrong to keep on living the way I am. Truly, if I don't make a change soon, I may lose my soul."

Poor Margaret! This desperate baring of her innermost feelings only caused her mother to break into a fresh storm of weeping, then to take to her bed for the rest of the day. Chrysostom was beside himself with worry over what had happened, and Angelica, too. As for Father Anthony, hastily summoned from his rectory at Verosvres, he scarcely knew what to say.

"Margaret, your mother's not a strong woman," he ventured finally. "Don't you realize such upsets as these are very bad for her?" Then, as his young niece stood looking at him in abject misery: "Child, do you want my honest opinion about the vow you made to the Blessed Virgin when you were a sick little girl of thirteen?"

Margaret nodded tearfully. "P-please, Father."

"Well, such a promise isn't binding at all, for it was made far too hastily, when you and your mother were both upset about your illness. That means there's no need now to worry about having to go off to the convent. In fact, perhaps you can become a greater saint here at home than you could ever hope to be by living in the cloister."

There were other things which Father Anthony had to say, especially about the value of obedience to one's parents and the sacredness of marriage. Margaret listened in dutiful silence, finally giving her promise that for the time being she would say no more in her mother's presence about wanting to be a religious. But in the days that followed, her heart was often heavy. How hard it was to have no one to understand her secret longing to belong to God! To feel that she was a constant source of worry to her family because she was so different from other girls!

"But I just can't get married!" she told herself frantically. "I . . . I can't!"

However, before the year was out, Margaret found an unexpected source of consolation. She had always loved children, and when Father Anthony suggested that she teach some of the poor little ones of the neighborhood how to read and write, as well as something of the Catechism, her spirits quickly rose. The birth of Chrysostom's first child, a little girl named Claudette, brought real happiness, too, and then the arrival of a second niece, Huguette.

In the year 1669 there was more cause for rejoicing in Verosvres. "The Bishop is coming here to administer the Sacrament of Confirmation," Father Anthony told his people one Sunday morning at Mass. "All those who have not received this great gift of God should start to prepare for it at once."

There was an immediate flurry of excitement throughout the parish. Owing to various political troubles in France, the Bishop had not visited Verosvres in more than twenty years. Thus, a whole generation of young folks, including Margaret, had grown up without having received the Seven Gifts of the Holy Ghost. Well, now this sad state of affairs was to exist no longer. Soon every eligible person in the parish would have the wonderful privilege of becoming host to the Holy Spirit in an even greater degree than at Baptism, and thus be better able to face the trials and temptations of life.

Twenty-two-year-old Margaret Alacoque prepared for the approaching great day by many extra prayers and sacrifices. She would take the name of Mary at Confirmation, she decided, and beg the Holy Spirit to be especially generous with His Gift of Fortitude. For surely fortitude, or strength, was what she needed in the constant struggle to live at home? To set aside the ever-present urge to give herself to God in the religious life?

"Dearest Mother, when I add your name to mine, please tell me what you want of me!" she begged silently. "Then give me the strength to do it..."

CHAPTER 7

THE FRIAR SPEAKS UP

POOR MARGARET! For a whole year after her Confirmation she was forced to follow her former way of life—and this despite the fact that she was now really convinced that the Blessed Virgin wished her to keep her childhood vow. But since Chrysostom steadfastly refused to listen to such an idea and Mama continued to try to arrange a suitable marriage, there was nothing to do but remain where she was. Then, in the spring of 1670, to celebrate his recent elevation to the Papacy, Pope Clement the Tenth proclaimed a special Jubilee Year. Every parish was to have a mission, he said, with numerous indulgences for all the faithful who participated in it. But this mission was not to be preached by the local pastor. No, experienced priests from the various religious Orders throughout France would visit each parish, no matter how small, in order to conduct the Jubilee services.

Presently a holy Franciscan friar arrived at Verosvres to open the local mission. All who could flocked to hear his sermons and to make their confessions. But soon the hard-working priest decided that it might also be well to visit about the countryside, bringing the Jubilee blessings to the sick and infirm who could not journey to church. To make this possible, he decided to establish headquarters in various farmhouses and to conduct his apostolic visits from there.

Madame Alacoque was delighted when she learned that the missionary had chosen to stop at Lhautecour. Aided by Angelica, she began a thorough housecleaning. Chrysostom, too, was busy about many things— especially the problem of seeing that the best of wine, meat and other farm produce were available. Nothing was too good for the missionary, he said. From his sermons, everyone knew he was a saint, and his presence at Lhautecour would surely bring the whole family many blessings.

The brown-habited Franciscan appreciated all that was done for him. However, after hearing the confessions of each member of the Alacoque household and imparting the Jubilee indulgences, he beckoned Chrysostom aside.

"Young man, I'd like a word with you," he said quietly. "About something very important."

Chrysostom's heart beat fast. Undoubtedly the holy friar, impressed by the family's hospitality, was about to show his appreciation by the gift of some precious relic. Or maybe an extra blessing. Perhaps, indeed, to foretell some great future happiness for the children of the household—little Claudette, Huguette and the new baby, Madeleine. . .

"Yes, Father, of course," he said quickly. "This way, please."

But once the two were alone, Chrysostom's heart sank. The face of the priest had become severe—almost fearsome!

"Father, if anything's wrong. . .if we've offended you in any way. . ." he stammered.

The friar looked at him sternly. "Selfishness is always wrong," he said. "Trying to keep for oneself what belongs to another is nothing short of stealing, my son, a sin against the Seventh Commandment. But when we try to steal from God—ah, that's a crime that verges on sacrilege."

Chrysostom's face turned pale. "But Father! No one here has ever done that! If they have, I swear to it that I'll. . ."

The priest raised a warning finger. "How old is your sister Margaret?" he demanded.

"Margaret? Why, she. . .she's twenty-three, Father. On July 22 she'll be twenty-four.

"Almost twenty-four! Then that means your family has been stealing from her—and from the good God— for more than ten years. Oh, my son, what a crime! What a truly dreadful crime!"

In vain Chrysostom tried to explain matters. The missionary would not listen. All things being equal, he said, deliberately to strangle another's free will in vocational matters, religious or otherwise, was a theft of the worst sort. No family could hope to prosper, either in material or spiritual goods, who stooped to such a sin.

"But Mama would die of a broken heart if Margaret left for the convent!" burst out Chrysostom finally. "You see, she's never been too well, Father. And so it seemed best—"

"Nonsense!" exclaimed the friar. "Doesn't your mother understand the meaning of selfishness? Doesn't she know that her children don't *belong* to her, and never will? That they've only been *lent* to her by the good God until they're ready to begin the work He placed them on earth to do?" Then, as Chrysostom stood looking at him in blank astonishment, the friar's

"SELFISHNESS IS ALWAYS WRONG."

voice softened. "Perhaps I'd better have a few words with your mother, my son. And right away. For the more I think of it, the more I'm convinced that God has sent me to Lhautecour for this very purpose."

Naturally Margaret never guessed the reason for the lengthy interview between the missionary, her brother and her mother. But before nightfall all was made clear. Pale and subdued, Madame Alacoque announced that she would no longer stand in the way of her daughter's vocation. Margaret might enter the Ursuline convent at Macon whenever she wished. A cousin of hers was already there, and seemed to be very happy.

"Of course Chrysostom would have to make inquiries about the dowry first," she said with a forced cheerfulness, "and also to see if the Sisters could take you..."

Margaret was close to tears. What a kindness the good Franciscan had done her in making possible this change of heart in her mother! Why, it was little short of a miracle! And yet it was surely not among the Ursulines that God wished her to be. The childhood vow had specified that she would serve Our Lady among religious especially dedicated to her honor.

"No, Mama," she said finally. "I don't want to go to Macon."

"But Margaret—"

"I'd like to be a nun in some place where I'm not known, where I have no relatives, where I could be just...just a nobody!"

CHAPTER 8

MARGARET FINDS HER VOCATION

DESPITE MARGARET'S expressed wishes, Chrysostom was soon on his way to Macon to arrange for her early entrance among the Ursulines. And a bit perturbed he was, too, over what he considered his sister's unbecoming lack of gratitude. After all, hadn't she been cluttering up the house and yard for years with young ragamuffins from all over the countryside in order to teach them how to read and write? Hadn't the Franciscan friar suggested that God might have some great work in store for her? A special mission which only she could accomplish? Well, what was more likely than that this should lie among the Ursulines, that oldest and most distinguished teaching Order in France, which now had a record of one hundred and thirty-six successful years in the field of education?

"If Margaret does have a holy mission in life, it's surely to be a teaching nun," he reflected. "She ought to be very happy as an Ursuline at Macon."

A mission for Margaret! The more Chrysostom thought about it, the more he was convinced that he was helping his sister to make the right decision. But when he returned home with the news that the

Ursulines at Macon would be glad to have her as a postulant, he found that Margaret was more than ever opposed to the idea. In fact, she had firmly made up her mind on two points. First, she would be a nun only in the Order of the Visitation of Mary, a community that was not originally founded for educational purposes but rather for prayer and reparation. Second, she would enter the Visitation monastery at Paray-le-Monial, and nowhere else.

Chrysostom was deeply disappointed, and so were the rest of the household. The Order of the Visitation of Mary was a comparatively new religious family in the Church, having been established only sixty-one years before by Bishop Francis de Sales of Geneva. Of course the Bishop had been a saintly man. Indeed, he had been canonized six years ago. There was also every reason to believe that some day his co-worker, Baroness Jane Frances de Chantal, would be canonized, too. But that Margaret should want to shut herself away from the world merely to pray and make sacrifices. . .especially in a convent at Paray-le-Monial, that obscure little town to the northwest of Lyons where she knew no one and would have scarcely any visitors. . .

"You can't do it," was Chrysostom's final decision. "Why, the strain and hardship would ruin your health inside of six months!"

Madame Alacoque was also possessed with similar fears. But remembering the recent stern words of the Franciscan friar against any further meddling with her daughter's vocation, she dared not express herself too freely. However, she did ask questions. For instance, why had Margaret chosen to be a Visitation nun when she had never met a single member of the community, or even visited one of their monasteries? Then, Paray-le-

Monial! What ever made her think she could be happy in that strange little town?

Margaret hesitated. What was the use of trying to describe the heavenly voices she so often heard in the depths of her soul—one that seemed to belong to Our Lord, the other to the Blessed Virgin? Or how recently, when she had seen a picture of Saint Francis de Sales, the Bishop had seemed to look at her with true fatherly affection, calling her his dearly beloved daughter?

"I . . . I just know I've chosen the right path, Mama," she said lamely.

Grumbling, Chrysostom finally agreed to take his sister to Paray-le-Monial to see the Visitation nuns. They would have an interview with Mother Margaret Hersant, the superior, he said, but just a short one. After all, there was no need to rush matters. Indeed, perhaps there was no room at Paray-le-Monial for new postulants. Or perhaps Margaret would change her mind after she had seen the place.

But on May 25, 1671, when twenty-three-year-old Margaret glimpsed Paray-le-Monial for the first time, she knew she had not been mistaken. It was in the Visitation monastery here that Our Lady wished her to fulfill her childhood vow. In fact, Margaret was so full of joy at actually seeing her first Visitation nun that she smiled and chatted quite happily with Mother Hersant.

The good religious, seated behind the heavy iron grille of the parlor, ought to have been taken aback at such evident high spirits. Usually, would-be postulants were somewhat ill-at-ease during their first interview. But there was something about this country girl with the radiant dark eyes that set her apart from all other candidates.

"So you want to be a nun, my dear?" she asked

kindly. "To shut yourself away from all that most people consider worthwhile?"

Margaret nodded vigorously. "Oh, yes, Mother! More than anything else in the whole world!"

"You think you could keep our rule of silence and prayer? Be obedient to the will of your superiors? Be poor and humble in all things?"

"Oh, yes! With God's help."

For a moment Mother Hersant was silent. Then with a sympathetic smile she rose to her feet and suggested that Margaret have a little visit with some other members of the community in an adjoining parlor. In the meantime, she and Chrysostom would discuss the matter of her vocation.

Margaret obeyed cheerfully. What a wonderful day! But how much more wonderful if she could be certain that she would spend all her days in this most blessed place!

"For this is where I belong," she told herself. "I know it!"

Later, however, when he rejoined his sister, Chrysostom was far from sharing in such enthusiasm.

"Well, everything's settled," he announced grimly. "You're to come back in twenty-six days, Margaret—on June 20—and Mother Hersant will receive you as a postulant."

Margaret's face was radiant. She had been accepted as a daughter of the Visitation! And here in Paray-le-Monial!

"Oh, Chrysostom, how wonderful!" she exclaimed.

The young man shrugged. He had now discovered that the Visitation nuns did have a small school for girls, but it was little more than a training center for future members of the Order and certainly could not begin to compare with the fine boarding school conducted by the Ursulines in Macon. As for Paray-le-Monial itself, it was the dullest place (despite its population of two thousand) that he had ever seen. Even the Society of Jesus had been unable to muster more than thirty students in the local college, and so had sent only three priests to be in residence there. In heaven's name, how could there possibly be a mission for Margaret in such a backward little town?

"Come along," he said dryly. "It's a long, hard trip back to Lhautecour."

CHAPTER 9

FIRST DAYS IN THE MONASTERY

THE TWENTY-SIX days passed swiftly. Then on June 20 (farewells with friends and family over and done with), Margaret found herself in her chosen home at Paray-le-Monial. Garbed in the plain black dress of a postulant, she was introduced to the thirty-four choir Sisters, the six lay Sisters, the six Oblates and three novices who formed the community. Then she was conducted to the novitiate—that part of the monastery which would be her home for the next year or so, while she was learning how to be a good religious.

"My dear, I do hope you'll be happy with us," said Mother Anne Frances Thouvant kindly. "The life will seem strange at first, of course, but don't hesitate to ask for help if you need it. You'll find everyone eager to be of service."

Margaret's eyes glowed. Mother Thouvant, the Novice Mistress, was every bit as understanding and sympathetic as Mother Hersant had been. And to think that both these good women had actually seen and spoken with the co-founder of the Order, Mother Jane Frances de Chantal! That Mother Thouvant, more than anyone else in the community just now, would help her to become a saint!

"Mother, I don't know what to say!" she burst out happily. "Oh, how good it is to be here!"

However, it was not long before Margaret's sense of well-being was shaken. In fact, her first difficulty presented itself that very evening when the community assembled in the chapel. For, one of the Sisters having read briefly from a spiritual book, everyone either knelt or sat with closed eyes and remained absolutely motionless for half an hour.

Puzzled, Margaret looked cautiously about. What did it all mean? What was going on? What was she supposed to do?

However, it was not until the next morning (after another and longer experience of the same nature) that there was the chance to ask any questions. Then, smiling, Mother Thouvant offered a brief explanation.

"My dear, meditation forms an important part of our life here. Didn't you know that?"

Margaret shook her head. "No, Mother. I didn't."

"Well, now you do know. Twice a day we meditate— for an hour in the morning and for half an hour in the evening. Be assured that these are times of many blessings, child. And great blessings, too."

Margaret hesitated. "But what *is* meditation, Mother? I just don't understand. . ."

Mother Thouvant could scarcely believe her ears. A postulant, almost twenty-four years of age, who didn't know the meaning of meditation? Incredible!

"Child, meditation is simply turning the mind to one or more spiritual ideas, then asking God for help to think about them profitably."

"But why is there reading first, Mother? Doesn't that rather spoil things?"

"BUT WHAT *IS* MEDITATION, MOTHER?"

Mother Thouvant gasped. "*Spoil things?* Why, my dear, the reading tells us what we are to think about! It gives us the ideas, or points, for our meditation." Then, as Margaret still looked puzzled, the Novice Mistress stretched out an affectionate hand. "There, child, don't worry. Meditation is really quite simple. All you have to do is to think of yourself as a piece of blank canvas before God, the Supreme Artist. He will make you into a wonderful masterpiece if you place no obstacles in His way."

Margaret nodded doubtfully. How stupid she was still not to understand! And how dreadful that so far she had misused the valuable time of meditation!

"I...I'll try to remember what you've told me, Mother," she said humbly. "And thank you so much for your help."

Mother Thouvant smiled. "That's all right, my dear. Run along now and ask Sister Frances to give you some work. After all, we do have other things to keep us busy here besides prayer, you know."

So Margaret went in search of Sister Frances du Challoux, one of her three companions in the novitiate, who lost no time in declaring that she had better help Sister Anne Rosselin with the sweeping.

"That child's only fifteen, and none too strong," said Sister Frances. "I'm sure she'll welcome a little help."

Margaret was delighted with the assignment. Yesterday, as soon as she had met Sister Anne, she had liked her immediately. Now that they were to work together, she would probably get to know her well. In fact, young Sister Anne might be able to tell her still more about meditation, and how to make one's soul into a blank canvas so that God might paint a beautiful picture on it.

But dear little Sister Anne was not of much help in

this regard. "Why, you just listen to the reading and let it sink in," she laughed. "That's all there is to it." Then, as Margaret stood looking at her doubtfully: "Oh, let's not talk about meditation, Sister Margaret! Tell me all about yourself—where you come from, your family, everything!"

There was no resisting the charming little postulant with her childlike smile. Before she knew it, Margaret was relating one detail after another of her former life at Lhautecour, including the fact that her youngest brother James was studying for the priesthood at the Benedictine Abbey of Cluny.

Sister Anne was more than interested. If James was twenty years old now, he was well on the way to achieving his goal. But what a pity that Margaret's sisters, Catherine and Gilberte, had died early in childhood and that there had been no others to take their place!

"Maybe I could do that," said the little postulant after a moment. "Maybe I could be your baby sister. Would you like that?"

Margaret's eyes shone. "Oh, I'd love it!" she burst out impulsively. "I've always wanted a little sister. . ."

CHAPTER 10

DIFFICULTIES WITH
KEEPING THE RULE

A WEEK PASSED, and Margaret experienced more happiness than she had ever thought possible. How good to be in the monastery! To know that in less than three months—on August 25, feast of Saint Louis, King of France—she would receive the holy habit of the Order of the Visitation of Mary! Then she would no longer be known as Sister Margaret but as Sister Margaret Mary. More than ever Our Lady's beautiful name (which she had added to her own at Confirmation) would be hers—but in a new and special way.

However, as the days passed, Mother Thouvant became worried over the most recent of her postulants. What troubles the poor girl was having with meditation! Repeated instructions on the subject seemed to be of little avail. She could not keep her mind on the matter, or points, presented to her in the spiritual reading. Then, too, she seemed to be drifting into the extremely serious fault of preferring the companionship of Sister Anne Rosselin, to the exclusion of that of the others in the novitiate—Sister Frances du Challoux and Sister Anne Piédenuz.

"This will never do," Mother Thouvant reflected one day. "All are equal here, and no one is to be preferred to another. I'd better speak to Sister Margaret at once."

Accordingly Mother Thouvant set out for the garden, where Margaret had been sent to weed the vegetables just a few minutes before. But when she finally came upon her young charge, the Novice Mistress stopped short in dismay. For Margaret, on her knees between the beans and lettuce, was lost in prayer, her face radiant! Nor did she give the slightest sign of life when called.

"What ails the child?" exclaimed Mother Thouvant anxiously as she made her way through the long rows of vegetables. "Sister Margaret! Is this the way you practice obedience?"

Once again there was no sign of life. Only when Mother Thouvant had taken her by the shoulder and shaken her somewhat roughly did Margaret come to herself. Then, dismayed and covered with confusion, she scrambled to her feet.

"Oh, Mother, f-forgive me! I . . . I forgot all about the weeds!"

Mother Thouvant was relieved, although slightly exasperated, too. "I can see that, my dear. But surely you know that we have a time for prayer here *and* a time for work?"

Tears of remorse filled Margaret's eyes. "Of course, Mother. But when I saw Our Lord . . . on the road to Calvary. . ."

The Novice Mistress stared. "*What?*"

"He was so tired, Mother! And covered with dust and blood! And when He let me understand that it was all because of people's sins. . .when He spoke of my own lack of gratitude and failure to love Him . . .well, I just forgot about everything else."

Mother Thouvant grew pale. "You saw Our Lord, Sister Margaret? *Here?* In the garden?"

Margaret twisted her hands nervously. "N-not exactly, Mother."

"Well, where then? Be specific, child!"

"I. . .well, I guess it was in my mind that I saw Him."

"And He spoke to you?"

"It. . .it seemed like that, Mother."

Suddenly the Novice Mistress permitted herself a slight smile. "My dear, you're tired and overwrought," she said briskly. "The hot sun's been too much for you. Come along back to the house, and don't worry about anything. Sister Frances will take over the weeding."

"But Mother—"

"There, now, there's no need to explain. I understand about everything."

However, in the days that followed Margaret's reception of the habit, the Novice Mistress anxiously admitted to Mother Hersant that she did not begin to understand the strange ways of the new novice. Although Sister Margaret Mary was humble, obedient and eager to learn, she simply could not keep her mind on her work. Time after time she forgot what she had been told to do. As for the manner of meditation laid down for the community by Saint Francis de Sales, she had not grasped it at all.

"Sister Margaret Mary tells me that Our Lord Himself is teaching her how to meditate," she reported to the superior, "and that it's useless for her to try to think about the points given in the spiritual reading. Really, Mother, I'm afraid this poor girl doesn't belong here at all. She's far too different from the rest of us."

Mother Hersant hesitated. Definitely Sister Margaret Mary was a well-meaning young woman, and very close to God. But the Visitation Order was no place for anyone who could not follow the simple way of life set down by the holy founders. Indeed, the real vocation of a Visitation nun could be summed up in one short sentence: "To be extraordinary only by being ordinary." Such things as visions, heavenly voices, private revelations, were definitely out of place, especially in a mere novice. If unchecked, they could eventually upset the peace of mind of the whole community.

"Sister Margaret Mary must learn to be practical and to obey orders," she said, frowning. "Meditation according to the Holy Rule is an essential. Now it's just occurred to me—"

"Yes, Mother?"

"That possibly a change of occupation would do Sister Margaret Mary some good, especially if it were in a place where she had to be thinking of others instead of herself. So what about in the infirmary, as an assistant to Sister Catherine Marest?"

For a moment Mother Thouvant was thoughtful. "Well, Sister Catherine does need help," she admitted finally. "And if you think you really want to try this experiment..."

"I do, Mother. Somehow I have a feeling that such a work is just what Sister Margaret Mary needs."

CHAPTER 11

THE CHEESE

ALAS FOR Mother Hersant's hopes! No sooner had Sister Margaret Mary been appointed to her new position than there were vigorous protests from Sister Catherine Marest.

"This novice is all fingers and thumbs," complained the infirmarian. "She spills the medicines, she drops the trays, she mixes up the diets. And she can't even apply a simple bandage properly. Truly, I don't know what's the matter with her, that she should be so clumsy."

Poor Sister Margaret Mary! Well she realized what a great trial she was to the infirmarian, and every day she prayed for the grace to do better in her work.

"Dear Lord, can't You help me?" she pleaded one morning as she started about her duties. "Remember when Mama was so sick with erysipelas and You heard my prayer and cured her? Now, please help *me*, for I'm so awkward and useless!"

But even as the young nun prayed, she seemed to see Our Lord as He made His way to Calvary, and suddenly her own little problems were as nothing. What sorrow in that Holy Face! What loneliness and abandonment! Why, it was enough to break one's heart to look upon this suffering Saviour!

Then presently Sister Margaret Mary gasped with dismay. Someone was shaking her roughly by the arm...

"Well, child, is this the way you spend your time? Where's that hot milk I ordered for Sister Pauline? Has it legs of its own?"

Slowly Sister Margaret Mary raised her eyes. Sister Catherine Marest was standing beside her, grim-faced and disapproving.

"I...oh, Sister, forgive me! I'm afraid I forgot all about the milk..."

"Forgot! Forgot! Child, is that the only word you know? Get that milk at once and bring it to me. Do you hear? At once!"

Confused, embarrassed and very close to tears, Sister Margaret Mary hurried off to the kitchen to get the hot milk.

She had failed again! What a humiliation! Yet, strangely enough, Sister Margaret Mary felt within herself a thirst for this kind of suffering.

So it was that Our Lord was to ask of Sister Margaret Mary an especially painful sacrifice. It had to do with something that the entire Alacoque family simply could not stand—that is, cheese. In fact, Sister Margaret Mary's feeling of loathing for this particular food was so intense that she had never been asked to eat it since she entered the convent! But now Our Lord was asking this sacrifice of her.

Poor Sister Margaret Mary! How disgusting cheese was! How positively sickening! And she knew that her stomach would feel the same way, too. "It would be a thousand times easier to die than to eat cheese," thought Sister Margaret Mary. "And if I didn't value my vocation more than I value life itself, I would be ready to leave the convent rather than eat it!"

"WHERE'S THAT HOT MILK I ORDERED?"

But there was no way out. The novice mistress wanted her to overcome her feelings about cheese—and so did everyone else. But most of all, it was God who was asking this big sacrifice.

So Sister Margaret Mary set out to eat cheese. But alas! She had to struggle and struggle with herself. She became so distressed that everyone felt sorry for her, especially Mother Thouvant. The struggle went on for three days, but Sister Margaret Mary was still unable to consume the offensive food.

At this point Mother Thouvant felt that enough was enough. Calling Sister Margaret Mary to her, she said, "I see that you are not worthy to practice obedience! I now forbid you to do what I had ordered you."

Sister Margaret Mary was aghast! She had failed to obey! It would have been better to die than to fail in obedience. What was she going to do now?

"I must either conquer or die!" she told herself firmly. "But first I must flee to Our Lord for help." So for three hours, in front of the Blessed Sacrament, she implored Him for the strength to overcome herself. Fervently Sister Margaret Mary prayed, "O Lord, don't let me hold back anything that You want from me!"

Then she said to herself, "I just have to get Mother's permission again. That's all there is to it." So back she went to Mother Thouvant to beg for permission to eat cheese! And Mother Thouvant gave her consent.

So at last, finally, Sister Margaret Mary forced herself to eat cheese. And it was every bit as bad as she had expected. Never in her whole life had she felt such a great loathing for anything! And the feeling did not disappear. For eight years she would feel the same way every time she had to eat cheese.

But after this, a remarkable thing took place. Follow-

ing Sister Margaret Mary's victory over herself with the
cheese, Our Lord redoubled His graces and favors to
her. Oh, how many new graces had depended on that
victory over eating cheese! In fact, Sister Margaret Mary
often had to cry out to Our Lord not to pour such a
flood of graces upon her, because she couldn't bear any
more! "Or else," she would beg Him, "enlarge my heart
so it can hold them."

But while these wonderful things were taking place
on the inside of Sister Margaret Mary, how many problems and questions kept coming up on the outside! For
instance, why couldn't she keep her mind on her work?
Why did she have to be so different from the other Sisters? Why was she unable to meditate according to the
Holy Rule?

Soon these same questions were also bothering
Mother Mary Frances de Saumaise, who had arrived
from Dijon in the spring of 1672 to take over the duties
of superior. Naturally the newcomer was amazed to hear
about the novice who had been upsetting the whole
community by her inability to keep the Rule.

"Why didn't you send the girl home long ago?" she
asked Mother Hersant briskly. "Visions! Voices! Certainly this young person doesn't belong in a Visitation
monastery."

But Mother Hersant was quick to defend herself.
Mother Thouvant likewise hastened to explain her
course of action.

"Sister Margaret Mary has really tried hard to be a
good religious, Mother."

"She's very humble and obedient."

"And kind and willing."

"Holy, too, in her own strange way."

Mother de Saumaise frowned. "A monastery is no

place for people with strange ways," she declared. "Tell this unfortunate novice that unless she shows some sign of improvement, we can never allow her to make her Profession in November."

This news was promptly relayed to Sister Margaret Mary, who received it with a sinking heart. Not to be allowed to make her Profession—that solemn act whereby she would give herself to God forever—was a tragedy of the worst sort. It meant that the good Sisters did not believe her called to be a Visitation nun. But hadn't she been plainly shown that this life was God's will for her?

"Dear Lord, don't let it happen!" she prayed.

However, all of Sister Margaret Mary's efforts to do her work well, not to forget orders, to meditate in the manner prescribed by the Holy Rule, were to no avail. She failed repeatedly as assistant to the infirmarian, and was finally dismissed from the post and set to washing pots and pans in the kitchen. Then came the dreadful day when she was informed that the community had voted against her Profession.

"Now what's going to become of me?" she sobbed, as she hurried to the chapel to pour out her grief. "What am I going to do?"

CHAPTER 12

PROBLEMS FOR
MOTHER DE SAUMAISE

FOR SEVERAL minutes Sister Margaret Mary continued to pray and weep in the darkened chapel. How dreadful to be a good-for-nothing! And then to be sent away from God's house! But suddenly the whole world began to vanish for the novice, as it had done so many times before, and once again she felt the Lord's living Presence within her soul.

"Go tell Mother de Saumaise that she need not fear in allowing you to make your Profession," came the encouraging words. "She is to trust Me."

Margaret's heart filled with joy. It was not with bodily ears that she had heard the Saviour's voice. Nor could she see Him with bodily eyes. Yet there was no mistaking the glorious message which He had just given her.

"Oh, Lord, I'll go at once!" she burst out happily.

However, Mother de Saumaise was far from being impressed when a transfigured Sister Margaret Mary presently stood before her and breathlessly began to explain what had happened in the chapel.

"Now, now, Sister, you surely don't expect me to believe that Our Lord came to you again!" she exclaimed. "Oh, my dear, why must you keep letting your imagination run away with you?"

"But I didn't imagine anything, Mother! Our Lord *did* come! I'm *sure* of it!"

The superior's eyes narrowed. Could it be that this poor novice was beginning to lose her mind? Frequently, deluded persons claimed to be on speaking terms with God Himself and even went so far as to issue orders in His Name. Of course the same was also true of many saints. But Sister Margaret Mary, with all her exasperating shortcomings, was surely no saint.

"Well, Sister, suppose you go back to the chapel and ask Our Lord if you can be useful to the Order by the observance of the Rule," she suggested dryly. "Remind Him that up until now you've been nothing but a trial and a distraction to everyone here."

"Yes, Mother. I'll go at once," came the prompt reply.

The superior nodded curtly, then returned to her work. But in a few minutes there was an eager rapping at the door and Sister Margaret Mary was standing before her again, even more radiant than before.

"Mother, I did what you asked, and Our Lord said that I'm to put the Rule before all else, and that from now on He will adjust His graces to the spirit of the Rule. Also, He says to tell you I shall be of greater use than you think."

Mother de Saumaise jerked to attention. "*What?*"

"It's true, Mother. Those were His very words."

For a long moment the superior surveyed the nun before her. How sincere she was, her dark eyes aglow with fervor. Truly, there was something special about Sister Margaret Mary Alacoque... And yet—

"My dear, I'm very busy just now," she said in a matter-of-fact voice. "Suppose you go attend to your work. Later I'll think over what you've just told me."

Slowly the joy began to drain from Sister Margaret Mary's face. "Yes, Mother, of course," she whispered. "I...I forgot I have things to do in the kitchen."

However, when Sister Margaret Mary had left (making a valiant effort to keep back the tears), Mother de Saumaise forced herself to face the truth. She had spoken somewhat abruptly to this strange young nun in order to test her humility for still another time. But as always, Sister Margaret Mary had passed the test triumphantly. There was no ugly defiance, no effort to argue. Only the wordless disappointment of a child unable to explain the meaning of some cherished treasure.

"No wonder Mother Hersant and Mother Thouvant didn't know what to do about this poor girl," reflected the superior. "Why, she simply defies description! In all my fifty-two years I've never had such a problem to figure out as this..."

In the end, after much prayerful thought, Mother de Saumaise decided that Sister Margaret Mary ought to be allowed to make her Profession. Finally, she persuaded the other Sisters, too. Thus, on November 6, 1672, twenty-five-year-old Sister Margaret Mary became a full-fledged member of the community, privileged to spend the rest of her days as a Visitation nun.

Sister Margaret Mary set out to follow rigorously the ordinary practices of the Order and the prescribed ways of prayer, as the superiors wanted. Our Lord was pleased with her heroic efforts, yet He still sent her special graces. And when she was pressed for an explanation, the answer was always the same. Our Lord had come again. He had been telling her how much He loved His creatures on earth, and what little love they gave Him in return.

"Love!" exclaimed one of the older Sisters to Mother

de Saumaise one day. "That's about all Sister Margaret Mary ever talks about! We don't love God enough in Himself, she says. We don't love Him enough in our neighbor. Why doesn't she talk about the need for a *fear* of God, Mother? That's what we should be trying to cultivate here, miserable sinners that we are. That's how we should be spending all our time."

Mother de Saumaise hesitated. Generally speaking, a fear of God was one of the first things that the Catholics of France learned as children. It was one of the customary topics for sermons, too, together with Hell and the ugliness of sin. But of course Our Lord had loved sinners when He had lived on earth, and taught them to love Him as well. Mary Magdalen, for instance, upon whose glorious feast day in July Sister Margaret Mary had been born. . .

"Perhaps we ought to ask Sister Margaret Mary to put down in writing all that Our Lord has told her about love," she said finally.

"All that she *thinks* He has told her, Mother," protested the older religious. "After all, who is to say these so-called visions are really true?"

Mother de Saumaise nodded doubtfully. She had long realized that no one in the community was sufficiently experienced in theological matters to pass a really competent judgment on Sister Margaret Mary. Not even good-natured Father Michon, the chaplain. But what if Sister Margaret Mary were to write the story of her life, keeping back nothing concerning the presumed visions? Then the manuscript could be given to various learned priests in Paray-le-Monial. Father Peter Papon, for instance, the superior at the Jesuit college.

"Yes, that's the best solution Sister," she announced finally. "Why didn't we think of it before?"

CHAPTER 13

"THE APOSTLE OF THE SACRED HEART"

WITH a sinking heart Sister Margaret Mary set herself to write a description of the many graces given to her since her arrival at the monastery. But even though she knew the task to be the Will of God (since it had been commanded by her religious superior), she found it almost impossible. After all, how could anyone really describe the beauty, the tenderness, the perfection of the Saviour? The joy that filled one's heart when He spoke? The sorrow when He made one understand how forgotten He was by the majority of His creatures? That even among those who did not forget, He was more often feared than loved?

"Well, Sister, just do the best you can," advised Mother de Saumaise. "And take all the time you wish. There's not the slightest need to hurry, you know."

So all through the spring and summer of 1673, Sister Margaret Mary labored slowly and painfully at her writing. Only a few of the older members of the community knew what she was doing, and these were not very much impressed. After all, Sister Margaret Mary was no scholar. Due to her childhood illness, she had had only two years of schooling with the Poor Clare nuns in Charolles. Therefore, any product from her pen could scarcely be expected to have much importance.

"Reverend Mother just wants to keep her busy at something," the Sisters told one another.

Then on December 27, 1673, the feast of Saint John the Evangelist, a wave of consternation swept through the monastery. Sister Margaret Mary had been discovered on the floor of the chapel in a dead faint! She had been as pale and rigid as a corpse when carried to her cell! Even several hours later, when she had come to herself, her few mumbled words made scarcely any sense.

"She's started calling herself 'The Apostle of the Sacred Heart!'" one Sister whispered fearfully to another.

"Yes. And she insists her own heart is no longer the same, because Our Lord took it out of her body, placed it in His own for a moment, then returned it to her all aflame!"

"Now she loves and yearns for souls like God Himself."

"Oh, but that's too much to believe!"

"Why, it's almost blasphemy!"

"It certainly is!"

"Poor Sister Margaret Mary! She must have gone out of her mind to say such things..."

Lying in her bed, more dead than alive, Sister Margaret Mary never realized that she was scandalizing anyone. All she could think of was that Our Lord had come to her again. He had invited her to rest her head on His breast, just as Saint John the Evangelist had done at the Last Supper. Then He had spoken with infinite tenderness:

"I have chosen you to make Me known to men."

What did it all mean? How was she, out of all the wise and learned people in the world, to explain to others about the Sacred Heart of Jesus? To explain how through this Heart, now living and beating in Heaven, He constantly yearned for love? How countless times a day His Heart was wounded through the sins and ingratitude of men?

"I...I can't do it!" she sobbed, tossing and turning in her bed. "Dear Lord, I haven't the words...the knowledge...the holiness..."

Mother de Saumaise (who had taken up a constant vigil in Sister Margaret Mary's cell) leaned forward anxiously.

"There, there, my dear, it was all a dream," she said soothingly. "Go to sleep now and try to forget about everything. You'll feel much better when you wake up."

But Sister Margaret Mary shook her head. "No, Mother. It wasn't a dream. Our Lord really came again. And He wants people to love Him...really love Him..."

"Sister, people *do* love Him!" protested the superior gently. "Thousands and thousands of them! Look at all the holy priests in the world, the good religious, the men and women and children who try to serve Him faithfully..."

Tears filled Sister Margaret Mary's eyes. "But it's not enough, Mother. Besides—"

"Yes, child? What else is wrong?"

"I'm *so* ignorant, Mother, so unworthy of making Our Lord known and loved! He told me so Himself. Then, some of the other Sisters..."

"Well, what about the other Sisters?"

"Our Lord is grieved because of them, Mother."

"*Grieved?*"

"Yes."

"But why, child? What have they done?"

SHE HAD HEARD THE WORDS, "I HAVE CHOSEN
YOU TO MAKE ME KNOWN TO MEN."

An expression of intense pain crossed Sister Margaret Mary's face. "They're not always faithful to the Holy Rule in small things, Mother. They give in to themselves too easily when they're tired or out-of-sorts. And some, because they remember who they were in the world, are inclined to pride. They even prefer their own will to yours many times."

For a moment Mother de Saumaise sat in stunned silence. Well she knew that some of her fellow religious were members of the French nobility, and that it was not always easy for them to remember that before God all creatures are equal. But that Sister Margaret Mary should have discovered this fact so early in her religious life, and seemingly through supernatural means...

"My dear, don't let any of these things distress you," she said with forced cheerfulness. "Just try to rest for the present. Later on, when you're stronger, you can put all this in writing. Then we'll talk about everything again."

Sister Margaret Mary managed a faint smile. "Y-yes, Mother," she whispered weakly. "Of course."

CHAPTER 14

QUESTIONS FROM THE PRIESTS

BEFORE LONG the community at Paray-le-Monial was more disturbed than ever. Sister Margaret Mary had experienced another vision in the convent chapel! This time she had seen the wounded Heart of Christ (apart from His Body) enthroned in fire and flames. A crown of thorns had encircled the Heart, and there had been a glowing cross above. Dazzling rays, brighter than the sun and transparent as crystal, had streamed from the sacred image, and again Our Lord had spoken of His love for sinners and His desire to be loved by them in return. Even more. He had promised to shed an abundance of grace on all who paid honor to His Sacred Heart.

Mother de Saumaise scarcely knew what to think, and was greatly relieved when Sister Margaret Mary came to her one day, very timidly, and announced that she had finally finished her writing task. To the best of her ability she had described all the favors and graces granted to her since her arrival in the monastery.

"Splendid!" exclaimed the superior, glancing curiously at the sheaf of carefully written pages. "I'm sure your little story is very interesting, my dear. I can scarcely wait to read it."

However, it was not long before Mother de Saumaise
was more distressed than ever. What Sister Margaret
Mary had written was interesting, yes. But so often it
read like the work of a great saint! Seemingly Our Lord
had made Himself known to this young religious over
and over again, and the Blessed Virgin, too. Yet how
likely was this? Wasn't all this talk about communica-
tions from Heaven more likely to be simply the result
of Sister Margaret Mary's own imagination? Or then
again...

"Perhaps all this is the work of the Evil One,"
reflected the superior, panic-stricken. "Perhaps he's up
to some terrible scheme to ruin the good name of our
monastery..."

But when the manuscript had been shown to Father
Francis, a scholarly monk at the Benedictine Abbey in
Paray-le-Monial, as well as to Father Peter Papon, the
superior at the Jesuit college, both priests hastened to
allay such fears. Nothing that Sister Margaret Mary had
written was against faith or morals, they pointed out.
In fact, much of it was wonderfully edifying. However,
it would be best for them to see and speak with Sister
Margaret Mary herself as soon as possible. Thus they
would be better able to render a fair and just decision
concerning what she had written.

"Of course, Fathers," said Mother de Saumaise
hastily. "I'll arrange for an interview at once."

Poor Sister Margaret Mary! When she presented herself in the convent parlor on the day and at the hour
appointed, she was suddenly overcome with unexpected
shyness. Even the simplest questions put to her by the
two priests left her troubled and confused.

"Now, Sister, there's no need to be upset," said Father
Francis cheerfully. "Just tell us what Our Lord looked

like when you saw Him. Was He a man or a boy? Tall or short? Sad or smiling?"

Sister Margaret Mary twisted her hands in nervous embarrassment. "I . . . I don't know, Father," she whispered.

The monk sat bolt upright. "You don't know? But you *must* know, Sister! Why, if Our Lord came to me, I'd never be able to take my eyes off Him! I'd remember every detail of His appearance."

Father Papon nodded decisively. "That's right, Sister. So would I."

Mother de Saumaise, fearful and anxious though she was, managed to smile. "There, my dear, don't be afraid," she prompted. "Remember, you put everything down for us to read, and very well, too. Now, just try to talk, very simply, about what you wrote."

Tears filled Sister Margaret Mary's eyes as she looked helplessly at her waiting audience. "When Our Lord comes, it's enough just to *be* with Him," she said slowly. "I . . . I forget about everything else."

Father Francis pursed his lips. "Well, then, how long does Our Lord stay when He comes, Sister? Fifteen minutes? Thirty minutes? An hour? Two hours?"

Slowly, forlornly, Sister Margaret Mary's head began to droop. "I . . . I don't know, Father."

Suddenly Father Papon leaned forward. "What's all this talk about honoring the Sacred Heart?" he demanded briskly. "Every part of Christ's Body is perfect and worthy of honor, you know—Hands, Arms, Feet, Head. Why should we pay particular attention to the Heart?"

"B-because—"

"Yes, Sister? Speak up, now. Don't be afraid."

"Because the human heart is the symbol of love,

Father. And if people today were to think of Christ's Heart..."

"Yes! Go on!"

"...then they might remember how much He loves them...and how much He wants them to love Him..."

For a moment all was quiet in the little parlor. Then Father Francis looked shrewdly at the timid young nun before him. "Sister, is it really true that Our Lord wants you to be the Apostle of His Sacred Heart?" he asked gently. "To make Him better known and loved?"

Sister Margaret Mary's lips trembled. "Y-yes, Father. Months ago He asked that favor of me."

"And what have you done about obeying?"

"N-nothing, Father."

"And why not?"

"Because I've never known what to do...or what to say to people..."

"But surely you've made plans of some sort, Sister! After all, if Our Lord asked a favor of me..."

Suddenly Sister Margaret Mary hid her face within her hands. "I'm not holy enough to talk about Our Lord!" she sobbed. "The words won't come, Father! Besides, I can't...I couldn't possibly...oh, I don't know what to do!"

Mother de Saumaise (deeply disappointed that Sister Margaret Mary was not giving a better account of herself before the two visitors), tried her best to console her young companion. But to no avail. By now Sister Margaret Mary was almost prostrate with grief. Then finally Father Francis rose to his feet. "I think there've been enough questions for today," he declared. "But if we could have just a few words with you alone, Mother—"

The superior nodded. "Of course, Father," she said

hastily. Then with a worried glance at Sister Margaret Mary: "Run along to your cell now, my dear, and try to get some rest. I'll come to see you shortly."

With a great effort Sister Margaret Mary lifted her tear-stained face. "Y-yes, Mother," she choked, and stumbled blindly from the room.

CHAPTER 15

OUR LORD APPEARS AGAIN

FATHER FRANCIS lost no time in giving his honest opinion of Sister Margaret Mary to Mother de Saumaise. This was a well-meaning young religious, he said, but not quite herself mentally. What she needed was more rest and plenty of nourishing food.

"Give her soup, Mother, especially vegetable soup," he counseled. "Remember the old saying: 'When the stomach is too empty, the head becomes too full.'"

The Jesuit superior nodded solemnly. "That's right, Mother. Soup will settle all this poor young Sister's difficulties. When she's been fattened up a little, there'll be no more of these so-called visions. Be sure of that."

Mother de Saumaise was both relieved and disappointed. There was no need now for anyone in the community to worry about Sister Margaret Mary. All that she had said and written about the Sacred Heart was only the product of a disturbed mind. In due course, on a generous diet of vegetable soup, there was every reason to believe that she would finally become a normal member of the community, able to fit in like everyone else. On the other hand, what a pity that her repeated statement that Our Lord wished to be loved

"GIVE HER SOUP, MOTHER..."

rather than feared was not to be taken seriously! Somehow there had been something wonderfully consoling about this doctrine. . .

"Still, the good Fathers know best," reflected the superior. "From now on, Sister Margaret Mary must have all the vegetable soup she can eat. And plenty of rest, too."

Poor Sister Margaret Mary! Of course she appreciated the kindly interest in her physical well-being, but the recent failure to convince the two priests that Our Lord had actually come to her many times was almost more than she could bear. Over and over again, as she knelt before the Tabernacle, she pleaded for forgiveness in having made such a poor showing at the interview. Yet even as she prayed, comforting words frequently echoed in the depths of her soul:

"I will send you My faithful servant and perfect friend. Confide in him. Fear not."

At such times Sister Margaret Mary always felt her heartbeat quicken. It was Our Lord's voice, tender and consoling! And in a little while all would be well, for He was sending some kind and saintly person to help her!

But the weeks passed, and the months, and still the promised friend did not come. Sister Margaret Mary hid her disappointment as best she could and tried not to be impatient. Yet it was very hard not to realize that by now several of the Sisters believed she was suffering from an incurable mental illness and so were inclined to shun her companionship; that others, fearing she had come under the power of the Evil One, thought it necessary to sprinkle her with Holy Water whenever they chanced to meet.

Then one day in the year 1674, during the octave of

Corpus Christi, Sister Margaret Mary's trials and sufferings faded into insignificance. For as she knelt alone in the convent chapel, gazing in silent adoration at the Sacred Host enshrined in the monstrance, the familiar surroundings began to vanish and she saw Our Lord more vividly than ever before. Garbed in dazzling white, a scarlet cloak about His shoulders, He stood looking down upon her with unutterable tenderness—His five Wounds shining like five splendid suns, His Heart aflame with heavenly light. Then came the voice she had learned to know and love:

"I will be your strength. Fear nothing. Rather, listen while I speak to you, and to the requests I now make...

"You shall receive Me in Holy Communion as often as you are allowed to do so, no matter what mortification or humiliation this may bring. More especially, you will receive Me in Holy Communion on the First Friday of each month.

"Every night between Thursday and Friday, I will grant you a share of that mortal sadness which I chose to feel in the Garden of Olives. This will reduce you to an agony more difficult to bear than death. You shall keep Me company in the prayer I then offered to My Father.

"In order to accomplish all this, you shall rise between eleven o'clock and midnight and remain prostrate with Me during the space of an hour, thus appeasing the divine anger by imploring mercy for sinners. In some measure this will help to make up for the bitterness I felt in the Garden because of the abandonment by My apostles..."

Sister Margaret Mary knelt in awed silence as her Beloved continued to speak. How kind He was! How good! How worthy of all one's love and affection! And yet there were millions of people who paid Him no heed at all; who never guessed how eager He was to give them His choicest blessings, especially in Holy Communion...

Thus, even when the glory of the Sacred Presence had finally faded away, Sister Margaret Mary remained in silent adoration in the chapel, motionless as a statue. Indeed, when certain anxious fellow religious presently came in search of her, it took considerable time before they could even rouse her to her senses. Then, wide-eyed and trembling, she tried to explain what had been happening.

"Our Lord c-came again!" she stammered eagerly. "He w-wants me to receive Him in Holy Communion on every First Friday...to m-make a Holy Hour of reparation on every Thursday n-night..."

The Sisters looked doubtfully at one another, then shook their heads in disappointment. Seemingly poor Sister Margaret Mary had just had another of her spells.

"Come along, dear," said one gently. "Didn't you know that it's way past dinner time?"

CHAPTER 16

MOTHER DE SAUMAISE
IS PERPLEXED

OF COURSE Mother de Saumaise was beside herself with dismay when she heard about the latest vision in the convent chapel. And when Sister Margaret Mary came to beg permission to rise at eleven o'clock each Thursday night to pray as Our Lord had prayed in the Garden of Olives, face downwards upon the ground, likewise to receive Holy Communion on the First Friday of every month—

"No, Sister, none of these things is required by the Holy Rule," she declared impatiently. Then, in kindlier tones: "Besides, haven't you thought what could happen if each one here suddenly decided to take upon herself this or that extra devotion? Why, there'd be nothing but confusion, child! Dreadful confusion!"

Sister Margaret Mary clasped her hands anxiously. "But Mother, Our Lord *wants* me to do the extra things I've told you about! He said so Himself."

The superior's eyes narrowed. "You mean Our Lord wants you to disobey me, Sister?"

"Oh, no, Mother! He told me to do nothing without your permission."

"Indeed! And what were His exact words?"

"'Do nothing without the approbation of your superiors and directors, for as long as you are under obedience, the Evil One will be unable to do you any harm. He has no power over the obedient.'"

"Well, then, my dear, everything should be quite clear," said Mother de Saumaise calmly. "You are *not* to interrupt your sleep on Thursday nights. And you will receive Holy Communion *only* when the rest of us do so—on special feast days of the Church."

Slowly, forlornly, Sister Margaret Mary's head began to droop. "Y-yes, Mother," she murmured. "I . . . I understand."

But when the crestfallen young religious had finally taken her departure, Mother de Saumaise could not banish the memory of the sadness in her dark eyes or the disappointment in her voice. What was to be done about this extraordinary young nun? she asked herself anxiously. Ever since her arrival at Paray-le-Monial three years ago, she had been the source of one misunderstanding after another in the community. But now that she was going so far as to suggest for herself the frequent reception of Holy Communion, even a Holy Hour in reparation for the coldness and ingratitude of men towards the Sacred Heart of Jesus. . .

"This is too much," reflected the superior uneasily. "I simply can't allow it."

There was a reason for Mother de Saumaise to make such a decision. According to the custom of the times, frequent Holy Communion was unheard-of for anyone in France, even in monasteries and convents. This was largely due to the attitude of one Cornelius Jansen, once Bishop of Ypres, in Flanders, who had taught and preached that human nature is so vile and corrupt that it should expect no mercy from God; and that the spiritual life should center around fear, rather than love. Fortunately, before his death some thirty-six years ago, the Bishop had recognized his mistake and done his best to banish this depressing doctrine from the minds of his followers. Even so, its influence was still being felt by many good people, including priests and nuns, who had arrived at the state where they dared not receive Holy Communion more than a few times a year, and then only in fear and trembling because of their unworthiness. More than that. The Jansenists (as the Bishop's followers were called) were also opposed to any loving familiarity with the Blessed Virgin or the saints. It was verging on presumption, they said, for sinners to approach these perfect creatures who were so far above them.

Now Sister Margaret Mary, divinely enlightened, was no Jansenist. And in due course the misunderstanding which Mother de Saumaise had feared broke out in the monastery at Paray-le-Monial.

"Mother, what *are* you going to do about Sister Margaret Mary?" exclaimed one of the Sisters one day. "It doesn't seem right that she should be acting so. . .well, so familiarly with everyone in Heaven—even Our Lord Himself!"

The superior hesitated. "There's not much that I can do," she confessed. "Perhaps in a little while. . .if Sister's health improves. . ."

"Oh, Mother, you *know* she'll never be like the rest of us!" protested another nun impatiently. "Even the vegetable soup isn't doing her any good."

"Why, the poor soul's much worse than she was, Mother! Imagine, believing now that she's holy enough to receive Our Lord every month!"

"To me, that's a really grievous sin, Mother."

"Yes, it's pride of the worst sort."

"Almost a sacrilege!"

In spite of herself, the superior grew tense. "But Sister says that Our Lord . . ."

"*Mother!* You surely don't believe in those so-called visions!"

"Not after what the good Fathers told you!"

For a long moment Mother de Saumaise was silent. "Well, sometimes I don't know what I believe," she said finally, with a helpless shake of her head. "All this is such a serious matter, Sisters. We mustn't make the mistake of being rash or imprudent."

But when the group had eventually gone their separate ways, a determined look crossed the superior's face. For days Sister Margaret Mary had been seriously ill in bed. Seemingly the disappointment of not being allowed to make a weekly Holy Hour, or to receive Our Lord on the First Fridays, had been a great shock to her and she was unable to eat or sleep. Soon, unless there was a miracle of some sort, she would be nothing but skin and bones.

"Well, I've had just about enough of all this," Mother de Saumaise told herself suddenly, rising to her feet. "If Our Lord really appeared in our convent chapel, if He really wants a devotion to His Sacred Heart, He'll have to send me a definite sign."

CHAPTER 17

MOTHER DE SAUMAISE
DECIDES ON ANOTHER PLAN

IN A few minutes Mother de Saumaise had arrived
at the infirmary, where she found Sister Catherine
Marest busy as usual about her numerous duties
among the sick. She found, too, that Sister Margaret
Mary was in an even more alarming condition than she
had been for several days.

"Truly, I don't know what to do for her, Mother,"
sighed the infirmarian. "She seems to be in dreadful
pain, although Doctor Billet says he can't find anything
wrong with her."

The superior hid her true feelings as best she could.
"Well, perhaps I can help a little, Sister. Would you
leave us alone for a while?"

Sister Catherine hesitated, then nodded doubtfully.
"Of course, Mother. But I'm warning you. Sister Margaret Mary is living in a world all her own these days.
She's not even likely to hear you if you speak to her,
much less give a sensible answer."

"Yes, Sister. I understand."

"All she does is lie in her bed, mumbling and stam-
mering about people not loving God enough, and how
necessary it is for her to receive Holy Communion on

77

the First Fridays."

"Sister dear..."

"I tell you, Mother, it's frightening. And a little exasperating, too. And in my opinion—"

"Sister!"

"All right, Mother. I'm going. But I thought you might as well hear what I had to say."

Soon Mother de Saumaise was experiencing the truth in Sister Catherine's words. Sister Margaret Mary, pale as a corpse and evidently in great pain, had given no sign that she recognized her visitor. Her eyes were closed, and her thin fingers clutched feebly at a crucifix.

"Lord, I've tried, but they won't let me come to You! They don't believe about Your Sacred Heart..."

The superior bent anxiously over the bed. "Sister! Sister Margaret Mary!"

"They think I'm out of my mind, Lord! Or that the Evil One has me in his power..."

"My dear child, listen to me!"

"Lord, what am I going to do? How can I explain to people about Your Sacred Heart when even the Sisters here don't believe in me?"

For a moment Mother de Saumaise stood in puzzled silence, gazing down at the frail young figure before her. Truly, the case of Sister Margaret Mary presented a real problem. Though her eyes were closed, tears were streaming down her pale cheeks and from time to time her breath came in such labored gasps that it seemed she must surely strangle. Actually the sight was such a heartrending one that finally the superior could stand it no longer.

"Sister, in the name of holy obedience, open your eyes and listen to what I have to say!" she commanded. "At once, do you hear?"

Wonder of wonders! Sister Margaret Mary immediately ceased her moaning and looked up. "Yes,
Mother?" she whispered. "You wanted me?"

As the superior gazed into the dark, tear-filled eyes
so obediently raised to hers, a pang shot through her
heart. Suddenly Sister Margaret Mary seemed so piti-
fully frail and wasted, far older than her twenty-seven
years! How was she possibly going to be severe with
one who was suffering so much? And yet, if there was
to be any lasting peace in the community—

"Sister, I have some important news for you," she
announced in a matter-of-fact voice. "I hope you're well
enough to hear it."

Suddenly fresh color flooded Sister Margaret Mary's
face, and she struggled feebly to a sitting position. "Oh,
Mother, do you really believe in me at last?" she burst
out.

"Well. . ."

"Y-you're going to let me make the Holy Hour on
Thursday nights? And receive Holy Communion on the
First Fridays, too?"

"My dear. . ."

"You really believe now in Our Lord's visits?"

With a great effort Mother de Saumaise steeled herself against the childlike joy rapidly dawning in Sister
Margaret Mary's eyes. "No, Sister," she said coldly,
"that's not it at all."

"B-but—"

"The truth of the matter is that I'm tired of your stay-
ing in bed day after day, of no use to yourself or to anyone else. And the other Sisters are tired of it, too."

Slowly the color began to drain from Sister Margaret
Mary's face, and she sank back weakly upon her pillows.
"I. . .I'm sorry, Mother," she whispered.

"MY DEAR, BEING SORRY ISN'T ENOUGH."

"Sorry! Being sorry isn't enough, Sister. Don't you think you owe the community much more than that for all the trouble you've caused?"

"Y-yes. . .of course. . ."

"Well, why do you persist with your lies then? Your foolish imaginings and day-dreams?"

"*Lies?* Oh, Mother, I've never lied to you! Our Lord really does come to me, unworthy as I am! And perhaps if you'd let me do what He's asked. . ."

Suddenly Mother de Saumaise drew herself up to her full height. "Very well," she announced grimly. "That's just what I will do—*if* you'll cooperate."

Sister Margaret Mary's eyes widened in tearful amazement. "Y-you mean that you'll let me make the Holy Hour, Mother? And receive Holy Communion on the First Fridays?"

"That's what I mean, Sister. But on one condition only."

"Oh, Mother! What?"

The superior looked sternly at the young religious before her. "On the condition that you get out of that bed and act like the rest of us. In other words, Sister, that you show you're cured—once and for all—of these miserable illnesses."

"But Mother—"

"If Our Lord really comes to you, tell Him to prove it to everyone here by restoring you to instant good health. That's simple enough, isn't it?"

For a moment Sister Margaret Mary did not answer, gazing long and earnestly at the crucifix in her trembling hands. Then slowly she raised her eyes. "Very well, Mother," she whispered. "I'll ask for a cure. Right away. . ."

CHAPTER 18

CHOSEN SOUL OR
MENTAL CASE?

FOR THE rest of the day Mother de Saumaise was
extremely troubled. Had she done wrong in
speaking so severely to Sister Margaret Mary? In
practically demanding of God that He show forth His
power and work her complete cure?

"I meant everything for the best," she reflected
uneasily. "Dear Lord, please forgive me if I've been
unkind. . .or acted unwisely. . ."

However, the next morning all such scruples were
rapidly forgotten. Then Sister Catherine Marest, beside
herself with joyful amazement, arrived at the superior's
office with the news that Sister Margaret Mary had just
left her bed, dressed without assistance, and now
seemed in perfect health. More than that, she was
desperately eager to be given some work to do.

"It's a miracle, that's what it is, Mother!" exclaimed
the infirmarian incredulously. "Why, this morning Sister
hasn't the slightest pain or weakness! And this, after
weeks of being at death's door! What on earth did you
say to her yesterday?"

Mother de Saumaise could scarcely believe her ears,
and immediately set out for the infirmary to question

Sister Margaret Mary in person. Surely there hadn't been a miracle at Paray-le-Monial! Surely Sister Margaret Mary hadn't actually been cured of her many ailments! But in just a few minutes—

"Yes, Mother, it's true," declared the young religious confidently. "I'm completely well now. No aches, no pains, no fever. Oh, how good Our Lord is when we really trust in Him!"

The superior gazed in blank astonishment. Why, Sister Margaret Mary was radiant with health! Her step was firm, her cheeks aglow with color, while her eyes— ah, never had Mother de Saumaise seen such eyes! A joyful light shone from their depths that was certainly not of this world. "Sister, w-what happened?" she stammered. "Tell me!"

Sister Margaret Mary smiled. "Well, Mother, Our Lady came and cured me," she said simply. "That's all."

"*Our Lady?*"

"Yes, Mother. Our Lord sent the sign you wanted through her."

"B-but what did she say, child? What did she *do?*"

"She blessed me with her presence for a long time and bestowed upon me many caresses. Then she spoke these words: 'Take heart, my daughter. I restore to you your health according to the Will of my Divine Son.'"

"Yes, yes, Sister! And what else?"

"'There yet remains for you a long and sorrowful way to go, ever upon the cross, pierced with nails and thorns, and even torn by scourges. However, fear not. I shall never forsake you, and I promise to accord you my protection.'"

For a moment Mother de Saumaise was unable to utter a word. Then slowly, she sank into a nearby chair and covered her face with her hands. There was no doubt about anything now, she told herself. Sister Margaret Mary must actually be one of God's chosen souls! Perhaps even a great saint! Therefore, what she had said and written about Our Lord's appearances could not possibly be the product of a mind that was sick or disturbed...

"Child, I don't know what to say!" she burst out finally. "To think how all of us here must have made you suffer when we refused to believe what you had to tell us about the Sacred Heart! That we even scoffed and made fun of you..."

"It's all right, Mother," put in Sister Margaret Mary hastily. "That's all over and done with." Then, a bit hesitantly: "And now I have your permission to receive Holy Communion on the First Fridays? And to make the Holy Hour on Thursday nights, too?"

The superior could do little but gaze in admiration at the radiant face of the young religious before her. "Of course, Sister," she murmured. "That was the bargain. No one here will ever stand in your way again."

However, Mother de Saumaise did not realize that several members of the community were still to have real difficulty in believing that God had chosen Sister Margaret Mary to foster a comparatively new religious practice in the Church: that of devotion to the Sacred Heart of Jesus. Thus, in just a few days—

"Mother, I do think you're making a terrible mistake in believing that Sister Margaret Mary is a saint and has some great work to do for souls," announced Sister Magdalen des Escures. "In my opinion, she...well, she's not really in her right mind at all."

"I agree, Mother," put in Sister Antoinette de Coligny, one of the older religious. "And if you keep letting her

make extra Holy Communions in such a condition,
you'll surely live to regret it."

Sister Claudia d'Amanze nodded vigorously. "Yes,
Mother. As for Sister's getting up late every Thursday
night for private prayer—why, that's simply ridiculous!
After all, if God wanted the members of the Visitation
Order to do extraordinary things like that, He'd surely
have inspired the Founders to say so in the Holy Rule."

"That's right, Mother. You see, we mustn't ever forget
that Bishop Francis de Sales had visions of his own and
is now a canonized saint."

"And he never said a word about making a weekly
Holy Hour."

"Or receiving Holy Communion on the First
Fridays."

"And neither did Mother de Chantal."

"So is there any reason now that an ignorant young
woman from the country should be setting herself up
above them and trying to change everything for us?"

Mother de Saumaise was silent. Well she knew that
Sisters Magdalen, Antoinette and Claudia were earnest,
devout religious, honestly convinced that they were acting in the best interests of the community. On the other
hand, they did belong to that age-group in the monastery which had grown up in the days when the depressing doctrines of Cornelius Jansen were being widely
circulated throughout France. Thus, since childhood
they had been taught to believe that God should be
feared, rather than loved; that monthly Holy Communion (such as Sister Margaret Mary now advocated) was
not in keeping with true Christian humility. Indeed, it
was verging upon a dreadful type of pride, they thought,
for anyone to approach the All-Perfect God so
frequently.

"Well, Sisters, I wouldn't worry too much," said Mother de Saumaise finally. "I'm the superior here, you know. And if I'm doing wrong in believing in Sister Margaret Mary and her visions—well, the fault must rest upon my shoulders, not yours."

Sister Magdalen shook her head doubtfully. "But Mother! Don't you remember what the Benedictine Father said? And Father Papon, too?"

" 'Sister Margaret Mary isn't herself mentally.' "

" 'When the stomach is too empty, the head becomes too full.' "

" 'What she needs is more rest and plenty of nourishing food.' "

" 'Especially vegetable soup.' "

The superior nodded curtly. "Yes, my dears, I remember. But what about Sister's remarkable return to health recently? How can that be explained away? Our Lady did come and cure her, you know, after I asked for a sign."

Sister Antoinette shrugged her shoulders. "Mother, I honestly don't believe the poor soul was ever sick at all," she declared earnestly. "She was just pretending."

"Pretending! But how could that be, Sister? You saw with your own eyes how terribly weak she was, not able to do the least thing for herself. Then in just a few hours, after she had prayed for a cure. . ."

Suddenly a look of grim determination flickered in Sister Claudia's eyes. "Believe me, Mother, you just frightened her back into her senses for a little while!" she burst out impatiently. "That's all."

Sister Magdalen nodded in solemn agreement. "It's true, Mother. Surely you've often heard how that can be done with people who are mentally ill?"

"Yes. Poor Sister Margaret Mary had a real shock

when you spoke so severely to her the other day. And
that shock was enough to put an end to her play-acting
for the time being."

"So you see there was nothing miraculous about anything. And the sooner you bring yourself to admit the
truth, disappointing though it is, the better off we'll all
be."

As she gazed at the three well-meaning religious
before her, the superior felt her heart sink. By now she
herself had become firmly convinced on two points.
First, that Sister Margaret Mary had always been in her
right mind; second, that she was also one of God's chosen souls. Only for the most serious reasons would the
permission already granted her to make a weekly Holy
Hour and to receive Communion on the First Fridays
be withdrawn. On the other hand, if these three good
Sisters continued to maintain that Sister Margaret Mary
was a mental case, and others in the community should
come to agree with them—

"Dear Lord, don't let there be any real trouble here
in the monastery!" she begged silently. "Holy Spirit,
please enlighten all our minds so that we'll know what
to think about Sister Margaret Mary. . .and what to *do!*"

CHAPTER 19

OUR LORD SENDS SOMEONE TO HELP

A LAS FOR the superior's hopes! As the weeks passed, the community grew more and more divided concerning the matter of Sister Margaret Mary and her visions. One group steadfastly maintained that she was a saint, and that it was a privilege to have her at Paray-le-Monial. Another remained convinced that she was not herself mentally, although quite harmless. A third, almost frantic with fear, insisted that somehow the Devil had taken possession of her, and that terrible things were in store for everyone if she continued living in the monastery. However, since she had made her final vows and could never be sent away. . .

"It's always best to have some Holy Water handy when walking through the house," the members of this faction told one another earnestly. "Then we'll come to no harm, even if we do meet Sister Margaret Mary."

"That's right. You know that the Evil One can't stand Holy Water."

"But keep your eyes open, Sisters, and be quick in using the Holy Water."

"Yes. The Devil is very clever, you know. He could let Sister Margaret Mary slip up on a person without the slightest warning."

Repeatedly Mother de Saumaise tried to shrug off this unpleasant situation, but with little success. As for Sister Margaret Mary, naturally her life soon became a constant martyrdom, made bearable only by the fact that she knew she was doing God's Will in practicing the extra devotions He had asked of her: the weekly Holy Hour and the reception of Holy Communion on the First Fridays. Also, when the whispered criticism and fearful glances of the other Sisters weighed too heavily upon her, there was frequently swift and unexpected relief. Then she heard Our Lord's voice, consoling beyond words, speaking in the depths of her soul: *"I will send you My faithful servant and perfect friend. Confide in him. Fear not."*

"My faithful servant and perfect friend!" Who could this be? wondered Sister Margaret Mary over and over. But the pathetic question remained unanswered. Then in November, 1674, there was great excitement in Paray-le-Monial when it became known that a new superior would soon be coming to the Jesuit college there. In fact, Father Claude de la Colombière* would arrive from Lyons shortly after making his solemn profession in February.

Father Blaise Forest and Father Francis de la Bonnardière, who, with Father Papon, had often been discouraged at the depressingly low enrollment of only thirty boys at the college, were delighted. Why, Father de la Colombière was one of the most promising young members of the Society of Jesus! For several years he had made a fine record as a teacher and preacher, not only at Lyons but also at Paris. In fact, he had even been private tutor to the two sons of one of the most impor-

---

*Pronunciation of Colombière: Koe-lum-bee-air.

tant men in France—John Baptist Colbert, Minister of Finance. He was also well acquainted with many other outstanding public figures, including the celebrated playwrights Peter Corneille, John Baptist Racine and John Baptist Poquelin (better known as Molière.) The artists Charles Lebrun and Peter Mignard, the architects Jules Mansard and Peter Puget, and John Baptist Lully, Director of the French Opera, were numbered among his acquaintances, too. Surely the college at Paray-le-Monial would grow and prosper under the leadership of such a well-connected and gifted young priest?

"All this is the best news I've heard in a long time," Father Forest told Father de la Bonnardière excitedly. "Imagine Father de la Colombière's being sent *here*—of all places!"

Seventy-year-old John Carrat (a lay teacher at the college) shook his head doubtfully. "The superiors could have made a mistake," he muttered. "Perhaps they really intended Father de la Colombière to go to Paris, not to a poor little hole like Paray-le-Monial."

But the superiors had not made a mistake, for shortly after his thirty-fourth birthday—on February 2, 1675—Father Claude de la Colombière arrived in town to take up his new duties. Naturally he received a warm welcome from his two fellow Jesuits, as well as from John Carrat, and soon had familiarized himself with all the places of religious interest in and about Paray-le-Monial. In fact, one of his first official visits was to the Visitation monastery, where his predecessor had already arranged that he preach to the Sisters on February 15.

Mother de Saumaise was completely delighted with the newly-arrived Jesuit superior, and even more so after his first conference. True, he was rather boyish-looking in appearance, and seemingly not too robust,

but how wonderfully eloquent! And how holy! In all her
fifty-five years she had heard few sermons, even by the
most experienced priests, which so stirred the heart to
love God and to do His Will in childlike abandonment.
It was indeed very fortunate for everyone in the community that such an apostolic young Jesuit had been
sent to Paray-le-Monial.

"Father, what about the Sisters' confessions?" she
asked presently, when she had tendered her heartfelt
thanks to the visitor in the parlor. "From time to time
it's customary for them to have a change of confessors,
you know. And I was wondering if perhaps you might
be able. . ."

Father de la Colombière nodded sympathetically.
"I'll be glad to help out, Mother. What about the
Ember Days next month—March 6 to 9?"

The superior's heart swelled with gratitude. "Splendid, Father. I'll inform the Sisters at once."

But as she prepared to continue her appreciation of
the recent sermon in the convent chapel, Mother de
Saumaise was suddenly struck by a strange look of
preoccupation on the face of the young priest before
her. Somehow he did seem dreadfully perplexed about
something, almost alarmed. . .

"Father, there's nothing wrong, is there?" she asked
hastily. "You're not ill?"

Father de la Colombière shook his head. "Oh, no,
Mother. "I'm quite all right."

"Good. I was afraid that perhaps the trip from Lyons
had been too much for you."

"Not at all. But on the other hand—"

"Yes, Father?"

"Well, I did have a rather unusual experience while
I was speaking to the Sisters today—something that's

THE MEMORY OF THAT FACE
WAS STILL HAUNTING HIM.

never happened to me before."

Then, to the great astonishment of Mother de Saumaise, Father de la Colombière proceeded to explain that there had been a certain young Sister among his listeners whose face had stood out from those of her companions in a most extraordinary way. Even now the memory of that face was still haunting him, for it had been intensely pale, and sorrowful beyond description. Yet there had been a glowing beauty about it, too, an almost unearthly radiance, such as he had never seen before.

Even more amazing was the fact that he had been able to distinguish unshed tears in the eyes of this particular member of the community, although the Sisters' chapel had been only dimly lighted at the time of his sermon, and separated from him by a heavy iron grillework. Who was that strange young nun who had been sitting in such and such a place, and whose tragic glance had all but pierced his soul?

Mother de Saumaise scarcely knew how to reply to the unexpected question. "Father, from what you say it must have been Sister Margaret Mary Alacoque," she observed hesitantly, "a young woman of twenty-seven who's been with us some four years."

For a moment the priest was silent. Then, just as the superior was about to launch into a description of Sister Margaret Mary's troublesome career as a religious, he turned abruptly toward the door.

"Well, this Sister is a chosen soul, Mother," he said. "Make no mistake about that."

CHAPTER 20

FATHER DE LA COLOMBIÈRE
BELIEVES MARGARET

FOR THE rest of the day, the superior could not banish this unexpected remark from her mind. How odd that Father de la Colombière should have been so deeply impressed by Sister Margaret Mary! As for the latter, she was beside herself with excitement following the sermon, for deep in her soul, even before the Jesuit had begun to speak, she had heard Our Lord's voice once again:

"This is he whom I promised to send you."

However, when Father de la Colombière returned to the convent on March 6 for the purpose of hearing confessions, the peace and joy inexplicably drained out of Sister Margaret Mary's heart, leaving it cold and empty. Suddenly she was overwhelmed with fear and self-distrust. It seemed entirely incredible that this Jesuit, with his splendid record as a preacher and teacher in two great cities of France, should be interested in what an obscure young nun had to tell him about the Sacred Heart. He would listen patiently, of course, just as Father Papon and Father Francis had done, but he could not possibly understand. Why, he might be scandalized, even angry, and might refuse to give her absolution...

"I can never talk to a stranger about Our Lord's visits," she told herself, miserable beyond words. But Father de la Colombière was kindness itself when Sister Margaret Mary entered the confessional. Divinely enlightened as to the identity of his penitent, he did his best to set her mind at ease. Wasn't there something she wished to speak about? he asked gently. Some vexing problem which perhaps he could help to solve with scarcely any effort at all?

In vain Sister Margaret Mary tried to control the strange fit of trembling which had suddenly come upon her. "N-no, Father," she whispered, "I only want to make my regular confession."

The Jesuit did not give up hope, however. "Come, Sister, something *is* troubling you," he said kindly. "I know it. Begin at the very beginning, now, and tell me everything."

However (as she would later relate), despite all her efforts Sister Margaret Mary just could not bring herself to unburden her heart. After Father de la Colombière had spoken to her for some time, she retired from the confessional in abject confusion. What a coward she was! What a fool! For months, even years, she had been longing for just such an opportunity as this. And now she had let it slip through her fingers...

"It's my dreadful pride that wouldn't let me speak out," she reflected tearfully. "Oh, dear Lord, can You ever forgive me? But I was *so* afraid of being scolded...or laughed at again...and of inconveniencing the other Sisters who were waiting."

Father de la Colombière was every bit as disappointed as Sister Margaret Mary that she had not been able to confide in him. Somehow he felt quite sure that he could have helped her in her trouble, whatever it was. And now it would probably be two whole months before he could speak to her again, since he must give retreats and conferences until mid-May in other places throughout the neighborhood.

"Lord, please give me the right words to say to this poor Sister when I do come here again," he begged silently. "Let me really help her, if it be Your Holy Will..."

This prayer was repeatedly offered by the Jesuit priest during the weeks that followed, and especially on that May day when he returned to the Visitation monastery in Paray-le-Monial. In the interval Sister Margaret Mary had also been praying for strength and light to confide in "the faithful servant and perfect friend" whom God had sent her. Yet, when she had the opportunity to speak with Father de la Colombière, the old doubts and fears immediately came upon her (as she later related), so that she could scarcely utter a word.

"I...I really don't have anything I wish to tell you, Father," she stammered.

Father de la Colombière spoke earnestly. "It's the Devil who's urging you to say such things, Sister," he said consolingly. "Come, now. Pay no attention to him."

"But I'm so afraid, Father! And the words—they just won't come..."

"So much the better. In such a state you can make a real sacrifice to God. Don't you want to do that—for some poor sinner's sake, if not for your own?"

Suddenly the fears and scruples which had been troubling Sister Margaret Mary began to fade away. A mysterious courage entered her soul, and soon she was pouring out the amazing story of all that had been happening to her, including Our Lord's repeated requests that she honor His Sacred Heart by making a Holy

Hour every Thursday night and receiving Him in Holy Communion on the First Fridays. Such practices, she explained, were to be offered to Him in a spirit of reparation.

The Jesuit listened to the extraordinary account with a fast-beating heart. Yet never once did he betray the slightest emotion, contenting himself with an occasional question. For instance, what did Sister Margaret Mary mean by reparation? Certainly she had been using that word very frequently.

"It means 'to make up for,' Father."

"To make up for what, Sister?"

"The coldness and neglect of all mankind. You see, Our Lord loves the souls He made so much! Yet very few ever think about that. Even good people are too busy about other things—"

"And you are to make reparation for these thoughtless souls?"

"Y-yes, Father. As best I can."

"And the other Sisters here—what about them? Are they to make the weekly Holy Hour, too, and to receive Our Lord on the First Fridays?"

"I . . . I don't know, Father. Our Lord never said anything about that."

For a moment the Jesuit was silent. Devotion to the Sacred Heart was nothing new, of course. Through the centuries it had been practiced by holy men and women of all ages and ranks, including Saint Anselm of Canterbury, Saint Bernard of Clairvaux, Saint Anthony of Padua, Saint Thomas Aquinas, Saint Mechtilde of Magdeburg, Saint Gertrude the Great, Saint Catherine of Siena, and, more recently, Father John Eudes, founder of the Congregation of Jesus and Mary. Yet not one of these chosen souls had ever suggested a weekly Holy Hour of reparation or the reception of Holy Communion on the First Fridays. . .

"Tell me more, Sister," urged the Jesuit gently. "What else has Our Lord asked of you?"

No longer embarrassed or confused, and grateful beyond words for the sympathy and understanding of this new-found friend, Sister Margaret Mary hastened to obey. Our Lord wished her to love Him, she said, since He was All-Good and All-Perfect. He wished her to understand that His Heart was a treasure house of infinite riches. But her own heart was not without value. On that wonderful day some eighteen months ago when she had given it to Him without reserve, she had suddenly felt herself to be pleasing in His sight in a new and extraordinary way. In other words, she had made a certain amount of reparation for the coldness and neglect of sinners, those poor creatures whom He loved so much but who never gave Him a thought. As a result, through the mysterious workings of divine mercy, He had been all but *forced* to give them the graces they needed to love Him, too.

"I know now that Our Lord and the members of His Church are like one big family, Father," she continued. "When we offer Our Lord acts of love and reparation, He uses them to give graces to other souls who need them."

Suddenly a rush of happiness filled the heart of Father de la Colombière. The great Saint Paul had often stated something similar, comparing the Church to a human body.

Ah, when the eye did its duty properly, the hands, the feet—all was well with the other members. But if there should be sickness anywhere—even a slight sickness—the whole body suffered. However, if the healthy members—those whose souls were rich in Sanctifying Grace—were willing to pray and suffer for those sick members. . .

"Sister, this is one of the most consoling truths of our Holy Faith," declared the priest earnestly. "Thank God that He Himself has told you about it!"

CHAPTER 21

TWO APOSTLES

A FEW WEEKS later, on June 13, the Feast of Corpus Christi, Father de la Colombière had fresh reason to rejoice. Then it was that Sister Margaret Mary announced that Our Lord had granted her still another vision. Once again she had seen His Sacred Heart aflame with heavenly light. The wonder had occurred as she was receiving Holy Communion from the hands of Father de la Colombière in the convent chapel. But this time she had also seen two other hearts in her vision—her own and that of the Jesuit. And as she had watched, these two hearts had gradually moved toward the Sacred Heart so as to be all but lost within Its consuming fire. Then Our Lord Himself had explained what everything meant.

"It is thus that My pure love unites these three hearts forever," He had said.

These three hearts! Father de la Colombière pondered the phrase long and thoughtfully. Could it be that he and Sister Margaret Mary were to bring people to know and love the Sacred Heart of Jesus as never before? That, in Christ, they were to be as brother and sister?

Sister Margaret Mary agreed that this was so. Also,

ONCE AGAIN SHE HAD SEEN THE SACRED HEART.

that neither of them had anything to fear, for such a union would be entirely for God's glory. However, it was three days later, on June 16, that still another wonder occurred in the convent chapel. Then Our Lord appeared to Sister Margaret Mary again, and with a truly startling demand. Henceforth, He said, she and Father de la Colombière were to work for the establishment of a new feast in the Church: the Feast of the Sacred Heart. On this day (the Friday after the octave of Corpus Christi), there was to be public reparation for sinners, particularly for those who scoffed at the Blessed Sacrament when It was exposed on the altar. The faithful would accomplish this reparation by receiving Holy Communion and then making a solemn Act of Consecration to the Sacred Heart. The reward for such loving obedience?

"I promise that My Heart will abundantly bestow special favors upon all those who honor It and who will win others to offer It such honor."

Father de la Colombière listened in awed silence to the heavenly message. A public feast in honor of the Sacred Heart of Jesus would be a splendid thing, of course. But how was this to be arranged, especially these days when so many people still believed (because of the teachings of Cornelius Jansen) that God wished to be feared rather than loved? Certainly to preach now on the theme that He actually wished to be considered one's best friend, instead of a stern judge, would scandalize many devout men and women. As for young people, who needed to be taught a certain amount of fear and respect for authority—

"Father, we're not to worry about anything," Sister Margaret Mary hastened to assure her spiritual guide. "Since Our Lord wants this new feast, I know He'll help to make everything possible. And just think! The date He mentioned—the Friday after the octave of Corpus Christi—is almost here!"

The Jesuit hesitated. "You mean—?"

"I mean that surely you and I ought to be the first to carry out Our Lord's wishes! Three days from now we should receive Him into our hearts as fervently as we can, then consecrate ourselves to His service."

So on June 16, the Friday after the octave of Corpus Christi, when Father de la Colombière had finished offering the Holy Sacrifice at the Visitation monastery and the community had gone about their day's work, he and Sister Margaret Mary knelt on either side of the iron grille separating the cloister from the public chapel and gave themselves completely to the service of the Sacred Heart. Of course neither could be precisely sure what God wanted of them. But what did that matter? Misunderstanding, persecution, suffering of all kinds, would be a small enough price to pay if, through their love, reparation could be made to the Sacred Heart of Jesus; if other souls could thereby be brought to love Our Lord as He wished to be loved—

Soon the Jesuit had become thoroughly convinced that Divine Providence had sent him to Paray-le-Monial for just one reason: to help Sister Margaret Mary promote a widespread devotion to the Sacred Heart of Jesus. Yet how were they to go about such a mission? The two ideas of loving God rather than fearing Him, and of receiving Holy Communion frequently, were utterly foreign to the times in France, so that it would be necessary to proceed with the utmost caution. As for the establishment of a special feast in honor of the Sacred Heart—well, for the moment this seemed little short of impossible.

"Lord, tell me what to do!" pleaded the Jesuit superior over and over again. "And don't let me make any mistakes..."

However, although Father de la Colombière set about his own part of the heavenly task with the greatest discretion, never referring to the Sacred Heart in his sermons except in the most roundabout fashion, he was soon the center of considerable argument. Townsfolk and religious alike were divided in their opinion concerning him, although both were forced to admit that he was a splendid speaker. And a holy man, too. But it did seem that he was rather young—only thirty-four—for the important post of superior at the Jesuit college. It was undoubtedly because of such youth that he had let himself be taken in by Sister Margaret Mary Alacoque, that poor deluded soul at the Visitation monastery whose so-called visions had gradually become public knowledge in the town. Why, now rumor had it that Sister actually spent hours talking in the confessional! And that Father de la Colombière believed every word about the apparitions...

"If this young priest keeps on listening to such fairy tales, he's going to lead countless people into heresy," one person told another.

"That's right. The Jesuits should have sent a more experienced man to be superior at the college."

"But Father de la Colombière is experienced! Just look at all the wonderful work he did in Paris and Lyons before coming here!"

"Of course. As far as that goes, why shouldn't he devote time to directing Sister Margaret Mary? It could be that she really is a saint."

"And a great saint, too."

"Nonsense! The poor young woman has been out of

her mind for years."

"That's a lie!"

"It is not!"

"It is!"

"It is not!"

"It is!"

Naturally Sister Margaret Mary was most distressed when word of the town gossip reached her ears. For herself, slander and misunderstanding no longer mattered too much. In God's plan, they were the price she had to pay to make reparation for sinners—and to bring many souls to a knowledge and love of the Sacred Heart. But that her spiritual guide should also have to suffer, perhaps to have his work at the Jesuit college ruined, and all on her account—

"Lord, don't let it happen!" she prayed. "Please don't . . ."

CHAPTER 22

FATHER DE LA COLOMBIÈRE
HAS TO LEAVE

A S THE months passed, her prayers seemed to be
answered in a truly miraculous fashion. The gossip and slander about Father de la Colombière
died away almost completely. Even Sister Margaret
Mary experienced a period of comparative peace. And
though little or nothing had been done to promote public devotion to the Sacred Heart in Paray-le-Monial, various religious at the Visitation monastery had begun to
take it up privately. Mother de Saumaise, for instance.
And the youthful Sister Anne Rosselin. Also a certain
Sister Marie Christine Melin.

Then one day in the summer of 1676, when Father
de la Colombière had been at the Jesuit college for
some eighteen months, Our Lord once more made His
Presence felt in the depths of Sister Margaret Mary's
soul. But this time the message He brought was on the
discouraging side. The Jesuit upon whom she had been
relying so much was about to be transferred to England!

Father de la Colombière could scarcely believe it
when Sister Margaret Mary told him the news.
England? Why, that was impossible! For years the
Church had been suffering a cruel persecution there,

so that now it was actually considered a crime for anyone to hear Mass or to receive the Sacraments. Of
course forty-six-year-old King Charles the Second did
have a Catholic wife, the Portuguese Catherine
Braganza, and Mass was offered regularly in the Queen's
private chapel for the sake of Her Majesty and various
Catholic diplomats. But it was not too easy for the aver-
age person to attend such services.

"Sister, there must be some mistake!" exclaimed the
Jesuit incredulously. "Our Lord can't possibly have any
work for me to do in England!"

Sister Margaret Mary, hiding her true feelings as best
she could, managed a slight smile. "You're going there
just the same, Father."

"But I thought. . .well, what about the work here?
The devotion to the Sacred Heart—the establishment
of the new Feast. . ."

"I don't know, Father. All I can tell you is that Our
Lord has need of you in England."

For weeks Father de la Colombière could not bring
himself to believe this. Then, late in September, all was
made clear. He *was* going to England—as private chaplain to Mary Beatrice d'Este, the young Italian wife of
James, Duke of York, King Charles' younger brother.
(She had become the widowed Duke's second wife
three years ago, when she was only fifteen, and had long
wanted a Catholic chaplain of her own.)

Actually, though, there was much more to the situation than appeared on the surface. For King Charles the
Second and Queen Catherine were childless, and on
the King's death the throne would naturally go to his
nearest relative. This was his younger brother, the Duke
of York, who had joined the Church a year before his
second marriage. However, certain powerful forces in

England were determined that this must never happen. Their scheme called for fourteen-year-old Princess Mary (James' daughter by his first marriage when still a Protestant) to marry Prince William of Orange, and then reign over England with this Dutch Protestant husband in place of her Catholic father.

"But we're hoping this plan will never succeed," the Jesuit's superiors informed him. "And largely because of you, Father."

Father de la Colombière stared in amazement. "Because of *me?* But I don't understand! How in the world—"

"Father, you're a splendid speaker."

"And with a great gift for making friends."

"You're a scholar, too, and well-connected here in France."

"B-but—"

"From time to time King Charles the Second will probably attend your sermons in the private chapel of the Duchess of York."

"Not to mention some of his most important political advisers."

"At first, of course, they'll come merely out of idle curiosity. Perhaps even to scoff and make fun of you. But after a while, with God's grace, they'll have a complete change of heart."

"More than that, Father. If our prayers for you and your work are answered, England will have a Catholic ruler even in our own day."

"King Charles the Second himself."

"And just think what that can mean to the Church!"

"There'll be no more persecutions!"

"Once again Catholics will be able to hold public office!"

"Even more important: because the English people love King Charles, his conversion will surely lead to the downfall of the heretical Church of England."

"And the return of the whole country to the Catholic Faith."

Father de la Colombière listened in stunned silence. His superiors expected *him* to convert the English monarch, a likeable enough man in his own way, but known throughout Europe for his worldliness and complete disregard of the Commandments? What a thought! Still, in virtue of holy obedience—

"I . . . I'm really not equipped for such an important work," he protested. "Surely some other priest. . ."

But the superiors shook their heads. "No, Father. You are our unanimous choice for the mission. In fact, arrangements have already been made for you to leave for London by the middle of next month."

Poor Father de la Colombière! It was with a sinking heart that he prepared for his departure, for he had no wish at all to live at the English court. As for Mother de Saumaise, she could scarcely restrain her tears at the thought of the community's losing such a fine spiritual director.

"How are we going to get along without you, Father?" she demanded in desperation. "As for Sister Margaret Mary—what's to become of that poor soul without your friendship and counsel?"

The Jesuit did his best to be cheerful. "Why, there'll be letters, Mother. As well as a constant remembrance in my prayers and Masses. Then again, who knows? These are dangerous times for any priest in England, even for those who live there by special arrangement with the government. It could be that I'll be back in France much sooner than you think."

But Mother de Saumaise was far from being comforted. Only the fact that the patient bearing of the present trial afforded a good chance to make reparation for sinners was of any consolation. Possibly if she and the other Sisters, particularly Sister Margaret Mary, were to accept this cross in the same spirit of loving abandonment with which Our Lord had entered upon His own sufferings in the Garden of Olives, they could merit sufficient grace to save at least one soul from Hell. . .

It was as though Father de la Colombière could read the superior's thoughts. "Yes, Mother, that's true," he said consolingly. "And don't feel too bad. Right now Our Lord is asking us to suffer a little something for Him— perhaps for a year, two years, three years. But later on He'll also be asking us to be happy with Him forever. Is that too hard a bargain?"

CHAPTER 23

WONDERFUL PROMISES
FROM OUR LORD

SLOWLY BUT surely, as the days passed, such childlike faith and trust in Divine Providence began to work something of a miracle in the soul of Mother de Saumaise. After all, who was she to question God's Will? As Father de la Colombière had said, all was going to be well—in London and in Paray-le-Monial.

"Yes," agreed Sister Margaret Mary on the day of the Jesuit's departure. "All *is* going to be well, Mother. We don't have to worry about anything."

However, some of the other Sisters found it extremely difficult to be so resigned to the loss of their spiritual director, especially Sister Anne Rosselin and Sister Marie Christine Melin. What a pity, they told each other, that the young Jesuit priest had had to be taken away! Never before had the community known such an understanding confessor. From now on, no matter who came to replace him, it was most unlikely that any Sister would be hearing of the need for a devotion to the Sacred Heart of Jesus. Either in the confessional or outside of it.

"And yet Our Lord does want this so much," Sister

Anne confided to Sister Marie Christine one day. "Father de la Colombière told me so himself."

The latter, a religious in her early fifties, nodded thoughtfully. "He told me so, too. And of course he must have learned all this from our good Sister Margaret Mary."

For a moment Sister Anne observed an uneasy silence. Naturally it was scarcely proper to discuss what had taken place in confession with anyone else. But since Father de la Colombière had usually avoided all public reference to the Sacred Heart devotion for fear of disturbing those members of the community who still did not believe in Sister Margaret Mary's visions—

"Sister, did Father ever tell you about the promises Our Lord has made in favor of those who pay honor to His Sacred Heart?" she asked timidly.

Sister Marie Christine smiled at the anxious young face raised to hers. Sister Anne was now twenty years old, but as innocent and lovable as the day when she had first come to the monastery, a mere child of fifteen, to give herself to God's service as a Visitation nun.

"Of course, my dear. I believe there have been six promises so far."

"*Six?* But I know about only three!"

"Perhaps Father de la Colombière never got around to telling you the rest of them, child, before he was sent away. But I can remember six."

"Please, Sister, what are they?"

"Well, as I recall, Our Lord has made these promises in favor of those devoted to His Sacred Heart:

"'First, I will give them all the graces necessary for their state of life. Second, I will establish peace in their families. Third, I will console them in all their difficulties. Fourth, I will be their assured refuge in life, and more especially at death. Fifth, I will pour out abundant benedictions on all their undertakings. Sixth, sinners will find in My Heart a source and infinite ocean of mercy.'"

Sister Anne's eyes shone with youthful enthusiasm. What wonderful gifts of God were represented here! And to think they were to be had almost for the asking! However, still more happiness was in store for Sister Anne, and also for Sister Marie Christine, when Mother de Saumaise presently took the two of them aside privately and told of a seventh and an eighth promise made by Our Lord in favor of those who practiced devotion to His Sacred Heart.

"Tepid souls shall become more fervent. Fervent souls shall advance rapidly to great perfection," she said solemnly. "That's what Father de la Colombière told me, my dears, before he went away." Then, by way of explanation: "Apparently some time ago Sister Margaret Mary put all this in writing for him. That's why he felt free to mention something about it. And why I feel free to tell you. After all, you both seem to have a remarkable sympathy for Sister Margaret Mary."

The two religious looked at each other in silent understanding. How true this was! And also how regrettably true that there was still a sizeable group in the monastery who refused to believe in Sister Margaret Mary and her visions! Honestly convinced that she was really a mental case, if not an out-and-out imposter, they felt that it was most unwise to put any stock in what she had to say about spiritual matters.

"Mother, isn't there something we can do to bring the other Sisters to a better understanding of Sister Margaret Mary?" asked Sister Marie Christine finally. "After all, you and I both know that Father de la

Colombière considers her to be a saint."

"And a great saint, too, Mother," put in Sister Anne eagerly. "Surely if you explained to the community about the eight promises. . .especially at a time when Sister wasn't around. . ."

But Mother de Saumaise shook her head. There was no need to do that, she observed. For the time being it was far better if the other Sisters' lack of understanding was accepted as a Heaven-sent trial, and borne quietly in a spirit of reparation. After all, hadn't Our Lord Himself set the example for patience in suffering? Time and time again, when His enemies had scorned and laughed at His teachings, he had maintained a charitable silence. Even when they had taunted Him on the Cross that He had saved others but now could not save Himself, He had chosen to suffer the agony of being a helpless human creature.

"He who could have had legions of angels to comfort Him, to vanquish every enemy and crown Him king, wanted to show us that suffering is too precious a gift to be thrown away," said the superior kindly. "It's the all-powerful key that opens Heaven for those who love God and try to serve Him, but which also (when offered up by his friends) wins the grace of conversion for those who hate Him, or who don't even believe in Him." Then, touched by the crestfallen attitude of the two religious before her, especially that of Sister Anne: "But there's always an Easter after Good Friday, my dears. And I'm sure that Sister Margaret Mary's Easter is going to be a particularly joyous one. So, let's leave it at that, shall we?"

For a moment there was silence. Then Sister Anne looked hesitatingly at the superior. "Y-yes, Mother. Of course. All the same, I was just wondering—"

"What, child?"

"Do you suppose that Our Lord will be coming again to make more promises to Sister Margaret Mary?"

"You mean in favor of those who promote devotion to His Sacred Heart?"

"Yes, Mother. That's what I mean."

"Well, now—"

"I've been wondering about the same thing," put in Sister Marie Christine hastily. "As far as that goes, it could be that He's already told things to her since Father de la Colombière went away that she's never confided to anyone."

The superior was thoughtful. "It could be," she admitted slowly. "After all, there's no reason why Our Lord should confine Himself to any set number of rewards for those who love Him. Perhaps He does have other blessings in store for those who honor His Sacred Heart—even more important than the eight which we know about already."

Suddenly little Sister Anne was all eagerness. "Oh, Mother, I'm sure of it now!" she burst out impulsively. "There *are* going to be more promises! And besides—"

The superior smiled indulgently. "Come, now, child! Are you trying to tell us that you have the gift of prophecy and can read the future?"

"Oh, no, Mother! Of course not. But the last promise! I'm sure it's going to be the most wonderful one of all! Why, it just *has* to be, after all that poor Sister Margaret Mary has suffered. . ."

"WILL OUR LORD BE COMING AGAIN, MOTHER?"

CHAPTER 24

NEWS FROM ENGLAND

SISTER MARGARET Mary did suffer a great deal in the months following the departure of Father de la Colombière for London. Yet she continued to have confidence in Divine Providence, and to make reparation to the Sacred Heart as best she could. Thus, every Thursday night, between eleven o'clock and midnight, she rose from her bed to pray face downward upon the ground in memory of Our Lord's agony in the Garden of Olives. Then, recalling His great loneliness at being deserted by all His friends, she forced herself to consider the terrible tragedy that countless souls were bringing upon themselves even as the seconds were ticking away in Paray-le-Monial. Misusing the great gift of free will, these poor people were choosing to spend their lives in sin, rather than in the pursuit of virtue. They were taking the easy path to Hell instead of the difficult path to Heaven. Worse still, unknown multitudes had done the same in the past, and in the future there would undoubtedly be many others to follow in their footsteps.

Only a single ray of hope filled Sister Margaret Mary's heart on these lonely Thursday nights. This was the knowledge that in the years to come the number of sinners going to Hell could be considerably lessened if only there were more generous souls to pray for them; to make reparation in a special Holy Hour and to merit extra graces by receiving Holy Communion on the First Friday of each month. Already Our Lord had frequently told her that she herself, by her own prayers and sufferings, was doing a great deal for sinners. But how much more could be done if only there were others—millions of others—to assist in such reparation! Men, women, even boys and girls, who were not afraid to give themselves to the service of the Sacred Heart by personal sacrifice. . .

"But how can they give themselves, when they don't know about the great need?" she asked herself over and over again. "Oh, Lord! Why can't You tell everyone what You've told me? Or, if that's too much, why can't people believe me when I tell them?"

Some nights there seemed to be no answer to these agonizing questions. Then again, on other nights, everything became quite clear. The saving of souls was a continual warfare, and, in God's plan, not to be accomplished without much sacrifice. But some day all the pain which Sister Margaret Mary was now enduring would result in the spread of a great popular devotion to the Sacred Heart. However, since the price for this glorious triumph had not as yet been paid, the suffering must continue. As a true lover of God, she must not look for any consolation now. Rather, she must try to practice great patience, and forget all about such things as human loneliness and discouragement. Above all, she must strive to have no bitterness toward those who were misunderstanding and persecuting her. In fact, she must think of these misguided souls as instruments of divine grace who were providing her with many precious opportunities to suffer and to make reparation for sinners.

Mother de Saumaise, now Sister Margaret Mary's loyal champion, agreed that this was the wisest course to follow. Nevertheless, she was frequently distressed over her inability to relieve what she felt to be an insupportable burden. Yet what could she actually do to help Sister Margaret Mary? Certainly it was useless to sponsor her cause openly. Too many of the Sisters still believed the young nun to be a mental case who only imagined that Our Lord had appeared to her. Thus, for the superior to insist on public devotion to the Sacred Heart now would only make for serious trouble in the community. Besides, love and reparation were meant to be willing gifts, never forced or grudging.

"We'll just have to wait a bit," she reflected. "It may take a miracle, but surely someday the other Sisters will come to believe in Sister Margaret Mary, too. Then we can publicly honor the Sacred Heart here in the monastery without any trouble."

However, despite their respective crosses, there were joys as well as sorrows for Mother de Saumaise and the young nun whom she loved so much. These were most evident when the mail brought letters from Father de la Colombière, filled with fascinating accounts of his busy days in London. The Jesuit superiors were in frequent receipt of similar letters, too, although soon they realized that their hopes for the conversion of King Charles the Second would have to be set aside for the time being. Deep in his heart the English monarch was friendly enough toward the Church, but seemingly he had not the courage to stir up political troubles by joining it himself. He preferred his present way of life, amid ease and luxury and boisterous companions, to the joy of possessing the True Faith.

But the eighteen-year-old Duchess of York, Mary Beatrice d'Este? Ah, hers was an entirely different story. Despite her wealth and high position, she was very far advanced in the spiritual life, and most considerate of the well-being of her new chaplain. It was a real privilege to have been given the guidance of her soul, and to try to comfort her in her many trials.

"*Trials?* But what possible trials could the Duchess have?" asked one of the Jesuits of his superior one day. "Next to Queen Catherine, isn't she the highest-ranking woman in England?"

The latter nodded thoughtfully. "Yes, Father. And young and beautiful, too."

"Well, then—"

"But she's a little Italian girl, and very homesick in England. More than that, she never wanted to go there in the first place, or to marry. From all accounts, her great dream in life was to be a Carmelite nun in her native Modena."

"And yet now she's the wife of King Charles' brother, a man of forty-three! What kind of a mixed-up story is this, Father? I surely don't understand it at all."

So the Jesuit superior set himself to describe, as best he could, the unusual background of the Duchess of York, whose spiritual welfare was now in the hands of Father de la Colombière.

Three years ago, he explained, fifteen-year-old Mary Beatrice d'Este had been living quietly in her native Italian town of Modena. On friendly terms with the Sisters at the Carmelite convent there, she had long made up her mind to enter the cloister at the first opportunity. But in that fateful year of 1673, when she was fifteen, a delegation of English Catholic noblemen had suddenly arrived in Modena to try to arrange for her marriage with a complete stranger—James, Duke of York. (The first wife of the Duke had died three years before, after entering the Church. He himself had become a convert a year later, but so far his two little daughters—eleven-year-old Princess Mary and eight-year-old Princess Anne—were being reared as Protestants.)

"I suppose the Duke was lonely, and needed someone to look after his little girls, Father."

"Yes. And even more important, the English Catholics wanted him, as heir to the throne, to have a good Catholic wife. So, after considering the various eligible young women of noble birth in Europe, they decided that Mary Beatrice was the best choice."

"But if the poor girl had never even seen the Duke. . . and if she'd made up her mind to be a nun . . ."

The superior shrugged. "Sometimes the rich and powerful are called upon to suffer in strange ways, Father. Little Mary Beatrice had no peace at all while the English delegation was in Italy. You see, they were earnest, sincere men, bent on a good cause, and gradually she began to wonder if perhaps she wasn't being selfish in persisting in her desire to be a religious. After all, her family and friends, even the Holy Father himself, Pope Clement the Tenth, were urging her to consent to be the Duke's wife."

"*Pope Clement the Tenth?* But surely he would never stand in the way of a religious vocation!"

The superior smiled. "Father, you're forgetting the very unusual circumstances. One hundred and thirty-nine years earlier, in the days of King Henry the Eighth, England had been lost to the Church. Well, here was an extremely good chance—"

"You mean Pope Clement felt that the Duke of York,

with a model Catholic wife such as Mary Beatrice,
might possibly succeed in restoring the Faith to
England?"

"Yes, that's what I mean. And finally, coming to that
way of thinking herself, Mary Beatrice agreed to make
the great sacrifice. She would go to England, marry a
man twenty-five years older than herself whom she had
never seen, and try to be a devoted mother to his two
little girls. And she would also pray very hard that God
would send her a child of her own—particularly a
boy—so that there would be a Catholic heir to the
throne."

For a moment there was silence. Then the younger
priest shook his head doubtfully. "But all this was three
years ago, Father! As far as I know, God doesn't seem
to have blessed any of the projects you mentioned."

"No, He hasn't," admitted the superior. "Her Grace
the Duchess has given birth only to girls, two sickly little mites who lived just a short time. Then again, it's
been hard for her to learn English, so that she's not
made many friends among the Protestants at court.
Besides, the damp northern climate doesn't agree with
her at all, and she's been sick a good deal."

The younger priest sighed. "Poor soul! No wonder
she's been lonely for Italy, and anxious to have an understanding chaplain."

With difficulty the superior suppressed a smile. "Ah,
I see you're beginning to admit that a Duchess can have
troubles!"

"Yes, yes indeed. But God willing, Father de la
Colombière will be able to help her a great deal."

The superior nodded cheerfully. "Let's hope so,
Father. And that he can help many other people, too."

CHAPTER 25

AN EXTREMELY DIFFICULT COMMAND

AS THE spring days of 1677 gave place to summer, Mother de Saumaise had several encouraging letters from London. In the private chapel of the Duchess of York, wrote Father de la Colombière, he was having real success in urging his little congregation to undertake devotion to the Sacred Heart. The same was also true of his suggestion that Holy Communion be received more frequently, especially on the First Fridays.

"It's a miracle, that's what it is!" the superior told Sister Margaret Mary eagerly. "Here in Catholic France, with Jansenism so strong, poor Father was afraid to stress these things for fear of being misunderstood and of giving scandal. But in Protestant England, despite all the bigotry and persecution of the Church—oh, my dear, isn't it wonderful the way things are turning out?"

The latter nodded briefly. "Yes, Mother."

The superior stared in amazement. "But Sister! Is that all you have to say? Why, I thought you'd be thrilled to hear such good news!"

"I am, Mother. Truly thrilled and grateful."

For a moment Mother de Saumaise was silent, shrewdly observing the face of the thirty-year-old

religious before her. Could it be that Sister Margaret
Mary was not feeling well again? Certainly she was
unusually pale, and there was a strained, almost despair-
ing look in her dark eyes. Possibly the fact that once
again she had been appointed to help Sister Catherine
Marest, the infirmarian, was proving to be too much for
her.

"Sister, you're not feeling well. Come, my dear, what's
the trouble? Tell me."

But Sister Margaret Mary shook her head. "No,
Mother, I'm all right. Truly I am. The only thing is—"

"Yes, child?"

"I. . .well, I'm still very proud, Mother, despite all the
graces Our Lord has given me. And. . .oh, what a miserable thing pride is! It's the root of all the sin and
wretchedness in the world!"

Mother de Saumaise could scarcely suppress a smile,
for in her opinion there was no more humble member
of the community than Sister Margaret Mary. "Now, my
dear, you mustn't let yourself be troubled by foolish
scruples," she said kindly. "Or wear yourself out at your
work. Why not ask Sister Catherine to let you have a
day or two off? I think that the rest would do you a
world of good."

"But Mother—"

"Yes, I know the infirmary's a busy place. But Sister
Catherine could surely find another helper for a little
while. Tell her I said so."

Very reluctantly Sister Margaret Mary went off to
avail herself of the unexpected holiday. But she did so
with a heavy heart, for not even to her beloved superior
could she bring herself to reveal what actually was troubling her. Yet how much she longed to tell her everything: how not long ago Our Lord had come to her

again, grieved and disappointed that certain members
of the community still refused to believe in His apparitions or to honor His Sacred Heart. And this had led
to faults against charity. Now Our Lord had declared
that Sister Margaret Mary must offer herself as a victim
for their stubbornness. But so far, fearful of what this
might mean, she had failed to obey. . .

The struggle went on. Our Lord continued to pursue
Sister Margaret Mary, urging her to make this painful
sacrifice of herself. For her part, Sister Margaret Mary
continued to resist, feeling she did not have the courage
to say "Yes."

Poor Sister Margaret Mary! As the weeks passed, she
grew more and more troubled. Unable to eat or sleep,
and realizing that her lack of obedience was most dis-
pleasing to God, she could scarcely drag herself about
her work.

Then, on November 20, the eve of the Feast of Our
Lady's Presentation, when it was time to renew the religious vows taken five years before, Our Lord appeared
to her again—stern and disapproving. Since she had not
made the private offering He had requested, He said,
she was now to make it publicly. On Our Lady's feast
day she was to kneel before the assembled community
and announce that she was about to become a victim
for their sins and shortcomings! Apparently she, Sister
Margaret Mary Alacoque, was pleasing to God, but certain other Sisters present were not. In fact, unless they
mended their ways, there was a good chance they would
lose their souls and go to Hell.

The stern command of Our Lord was almost more
than Sister Margaret Mary could bear. All she could say
was, "My God, have pity on me according to the great-
ness of Thy mercy!" Half-fainting, she sank upon the

ground and remained there until found by some of the other Sisters. These, believing that she was seriously ill, would have carried her to her cell, but Sister Margaret Mary roused herself and insisted on being taken to see Mother de Saumaise.

"But she's sick in bed today," was the somewhat impatient protest. "It wouldn't be right to bother her now, Sister. Perhaps tomorrow—"

However, Sister Margaret Mary was desperate. She *must* speak to the superior! Something terrible had just happened...she needed a special permission...Our Lord was disappointed, even angry...certain souls were in grave danger...there was no time to lose...

Naturally Mother de Saumaise was greatly distressed when she heard the complete story, and only reluctantly gave permission for Sister Margaret Mary to make the public offering of herself on Our Lady's feast.

"A victim for the sins of the community!" she whispered to herself, shuddering, when the weeping young nun had finally been led away. "Poor child, who's ever going to believe that?"

The superior's fears were fully justified, for the next day, when Sister Margaret Mary had knelt before the assembled community and delivered Our Lord's message—trembling and scarcely able to speak—indignation ran high in the monastery. Some of the Sisters were particularly annoyed. This was too much, they declared. Who was Sister Margaret Mary Alacoque to set herself up as a model of Christian virtue? Just thirty years old (and only six years a religious), she would be far better off if she concentrated on keeping the Holy Rule and refrained from criticizing other Sisters whose years in religion amounted to nearly a lifetime.

"Reverend Mother should have known better than to

SHE MUST OFFER HERSELF AS A VICTIM...

allow this disgraceful performance!"

"Yes, indeed. As far as that goes, if Sister Margaret Mary is holy enough for God to choose her as a victim soul, why couldn't she have worked a miracle two years ago and cured her sick mother, instead of letting the poor woman die?"

"And her uncle, Father Anthony, last year!"

"Her brother Chrysostom's wife isn't too well these days either, but what's she doing for her?"

"Why, nothing! Absolutely nothing!"

"Then what about her own self? If she were a real saint, would she be disrupting our community with all this talk about heavenly voices?"

"Of course not. She'd just go about her duties quietly like everyone else."

"Really, everyone's been far too lenient with this young woman."

"Especially Mother de Saumaise."

"That's right. Poor soul, she meant well, of course, but she's only succeeded in spoiling her."

To the best of her ability the superior tried to ignore these criticisms. As for Sister Margaret Mary, she could scarcely bear to think about what had happened on Our Lady's feast day. Never in all her life had she suffered such agony! Yet the next day, after the painful episode was over, Our Lord revealed to Sister Margaret Mary that His justice was now satisfied.

Yes, if this suffering had been what Our Lord wanted of her. . .if somehow it had helped to pay the price to promote the glory of God—by establishing the reign of the Sacred Heart in the hearts of men. . .with many people observing the Holy Hour on Thursday nights and receiving Holy Communion in loving reparation on the First Fridays. . .

"Nothing would be too much to ask for a grace like that," she realized soberly. "Nothing in the whole world!"

CHAPTER 26

PRECIOUS CROSSES

IN FARAWAY London, Father de la Colombière was also being called upon to pay his part of the price that someday would make possible a general devotion to the Sacred Heart of Jesus. And the Duke and Duchess of York as well. For on November 4 of that same year, 1677, they had been powerless to prevent the marriage of fifteen-year-old Princess Mary to Prince William of Orange. The girl had spent the greater part of her wedding day in tears, for she was devoted to her father and stepmother, and had no wish to leave for Holland with a man she scarcely knew. Or some day to be ruler of England in place of her Catholic father. Yet such was her duty, announced King Charles the Second and his Protestant advisers. Why, if she should fail to persevere in the Protestant religion in which she had been born, or to marry Prince William, there might be an immediate uprising in England, with thousands of innocent people losing their lives!

Two weeks later, on November 18, the anxiety of the Duke and Duchess over the Princess' marriage was partially forgotten when they became the proud parents of their third child, a baby boy, the long-awaited Prince

of Wales. Naturally the English Catholics went wild
with joy, for now the throne could someday go to the
new baby, who would be reared a Catholic, instead of
to Princess Mary and her Protestant husband. But their
joy was to be short-lived. Five weeks later, on December 22, the tiny royal infant, never strong, went to join
his two little sisters in Heaven.

"I write only to snatch a moment of consolation with
you, and to tell you of the death of the little prince
whom God had given us," wrote Father de la
Colombière to Mother de Saumaise. "This has been a
great tragedy to all Catholics, but most of all to his
father and mother. However, they have received the loss
in the most Christian way in the world."

Sister Margaret Mary was not surprised at the new
sorrow just befallen nineteen-year-old Mary Beatrice
d'Este and her forty-four-year-old husband. Gradually
she had come to realize that the price to be paid for
a widespread interest in reparation to the Sacred
Heart—especially through the Holy Hour and the
reception of Holy Communion on the First Fridays—
was an enormous one. Each was a powerful means
for the salvation and sanctification of souls, against
which Satan seemed to be waging a steadily increasing
warfare. But the willing return of the English people
to the Church under the Duke of York or a child of
his by the Duchess, or under some future Catholic
ruler? Ah, the price for this grace was far greater! Truly
beyond all imagining! Generations might have to pass,
even centuries, before it was paid.

Then some five months later, in May, 1678, there
was fresh cause for concern for Sister Margaret Mary.
The six-year term of office of Mother de Saumaise now
having come to an end, this beloved superior was being

recalled to Dijon and her place at Paray-le-Monial taken by Mother Péronne Rosalie Greyfié.

Mother Greyfié, a devout but thoroughly unimaginative and practical woman of forty years, was far from enthusiastic when some of the older Sisters began to relate the extraordinary story of Sister Margaret Mary and her visions. And she was even less pleased when she discovered that for some time the whole situation had been causing an ever-growing tension in the community, even downright unpleasantness.

"Why, this is disgraceful!" she burst out. "We simply can't have such goings-on here, Sisters. Suppose news of all these weird things should leak out in the town?"

Sister Magdalen des Escures shrugged her shoulders. "*Suppose*, Mother? Why, it did that long ago! Now everyone knows about Sister Margaret Mary and all the trouble she's been causing."

Sister Antoinette de Coligny agreed. "They certainly do. Why, from time to time I've even seen some of them creep into the public chapel to try to watch her at prayer through the iron grille."

"Yes," sniffed Sister Claudia d'Amanze. "The poor souls have a vain hope that she'll be granted a vision while they're there. I tell you, Mother, some days there's no more privacy in this monastery than if we were running a circus!"

A grim light flickered in the new superior's eyes. "Well, we'll soon put a stop to all this," she declared abruptly. "And to anything else that isn't in complete accordance with the Holy Rule."

Poor Sister Margaret Mary! Within just a few days her heart was well-nigh broken, for then it was that Mother Greyfié suddenly ordered her to give up the weekly

Holy Hour and to remain in bed on Thursday nights like everyone else. Apparently the infirmarian had complained that her helper was not getting sufficient rest to maintain strength, and so was of little use in caring for the sick.

"But Mother, Our Lord *wants* me to make reparation in a special Holy Hour!" protested Sister Margaret Mary respectfully. "He told me so Himself! Every Thursday night, He said, from eleven o'clock until midnight..."

"Our Lord has also sent me here to see that you take care of your health and perform your various duties," replied Mother Greyfié calmly. "Or don't you believe that, Sister?"

"Oh, Mother, of course! But—"

"Then, in view of your vow of obedience, what are you going to do?"

Tears filled Sister Margaret Mary's eyes. There was only one answer to that question, as Our Lord had explained long ago.

"Whatever you tell me, Mother. Of course."

Mother Greyfié, a bit taken back at such childlike simplicity, nodded approvingly. "Very good, Sister. I'm glad to see you haven't forgotten that obedience is a most important virtue for a religious. Without it, real progress in the other virtues is next to impossible."

However, despite frequent meditation on the virtue of obedience, Sister Margaret Mary found her new cross very hard to bear. It was even more painful that from time to time Our Lord appeared to her and complained about her failure to keep Him company in the special Holy Hour He had requested. Also, there was the distressing news that the health of Father de la Colombière was failing and that soon he would be called upon to suffer a great deal. In fact, within the next few weeks he would experience more trials and troubles than he had ever known in his whole life.

For several days Sister Margaret Mary bravely struggled to bear the pain caused by this secret knowledge. Then one morning, unable to contain herself any longer, she sought out Mother Greyfié and earnestly begged permission to resume the Holy Hour. Her health would not suffer, she promised, and it was most important that someone make reparation for sinners. Otherwise Divine Justice might have to seek a victim elsewhere, perhaps in the community itself.

Mother Greyfié hesitated. She had no wish to be unkind, and in spite of herself she was somehow impressed with this earnest young nun before her. Perhaps after all it would do no harm to allow her an extra hour of prayer once a week? Perhaps this was just what she needed to settle her spirits and make her of some real use about the house? However, remembering the repeated complaints that Sister Margaret Mary was none too strong and needed all the rest she could get—

"No, Sister," she said finally, "a Holy Hour such as you've been accustomed to make is not part of our Rule." Then, in more kindly tones: "Oh, my dear, why do you have to be so different from the rest of us? For instance, why can't you be more like Sister Mary Elizabeth Quarré? Simple, obedient, hard-working, dependable, that child never gives me the slightest cause for concern."

Sister Margaret Mary lowered her eyes. What was the use of trying to explain anything to this new superior? Seemingly it was Our Lord's wish that, for the time being, she, like so many others in the community, should fail to see the great need for reparation to the Sacred Heart of Jesus.

"Oh, Mother, I'm sorry I troubled you!" she burst out contritely. "And you're quite right about Sister Mary Elizabeth's being a wonderful religious. With God's help, I must try to watch her more closely and to learn from her all that I can..."

CHAPTER 27

FATHER DE LA COLOMBIÈRE
IN PRISON

A S THE weeks passed, Sister Margaret Mary did make a valiant effort to model herself on the youthful religious who was so pleasing to Mother Greyfié. And to be of real use in the infirmary, too, so that Sister Catherine Marest would have no cause for complaint. Yet her heart was heavy. Repeatedly these days Our Lord was confiding to her that in London things were not going at all well with Father de la Colombière. He was working as hard as ever, of course, and making many converts to the True Faith. He had also induced a large number of men and women to practice devotion to the Sacred Heart, including the Duke and Duchess of York and members of their household. But recently tuberculosis had struck him down. More than that, all his efforts to convert King Charles the Second had come to naught. The English ruler was secretly partial to the Faith, but fearful of doing anything that might cost him his throne. Also, he had lived in sinful luxury for so many years that he had really ceased to have much interest in spiritual matters.

Although not gifted with any heavenly revelations, the French superiors of Father de la Colombière knew all about what was going on at the English court. Reluctantly they had come to realize that the forces of evil were still hard at work there, spreading lies and scandal about the Church. Indeed, there was now a malicious rumor afloat that the Holy Father himself, Pope Innocent the Eleventh, would like nothing better than to be sovereign of England! Already, it was said, he had many spies working for him in London, especially priests. As for the Catholic ruler of France, Louis the Fourteenth, the word was that he also had designs upon the island kingdom. And what would happen if either the Pope's forces or those of King Louis should launch a successful invasion? Why, every English Protestant would be cruelly murdered and all his property seized! Truly, it was no longer possible for any loyal Englishman to sleep soundly in his bed at night for fear of these two foreign tyrants...

"The Devil is certainly busy these days," the Jesuit superiors told one another anxiously in the summer of 1678, "especially in England. And from the looks of things, he's going to be busier still. Perhaps, in view of Father de la Colombiére's poor health, we ought to bring him back to France?"

However, when approached about the matter, the zealous chaplain replied that he did not wish to come home for health reasons or because of any political danger because of his being a Frenchman and a priest. If the superiors were willing, he much preferred to stay where he was. Of course, it was true that in fall and winter the English climate was abominable, with the chill fog and dampness penetrating one's very bones. And to a Frenchman, the food was uninteresting. But what did personal comfort matter when one was working for souls? Besides, he was still a comparatively young man—only thirty-seven. God willing, there would be plenty of time in the future to return to sunny France with its good wines and deliciously cooked meals.

The nineteen-year-old Duchess of York was not so sure of this, however, especially when September came to England. For several weeks an Anglican clergyman, one Titus Oates, a particularly malicious enemy of the Church, had been stirring up public opinion against the English Catholics. A plot was on foot, he bellowed, whereby these troublemakers planned to murder King Charles the Second and then place the Pope's tool, the Duke of York, on the throne. Benedictines, Franciscans, Jesuits, even several members of the House of Lords were deeply involved. Without exception, these wretched traitors must be arrested at once and condemned to death.

"It's all too ridiculous!" Mary Beatrice told Father de la Colombière one day, after a short trip to Holland where she had been visiting her stepdaughter, Princess Mary. "And yet—oh, I'm *so* afraid! For these good priests and their friends, for my husband, myself, and for you, too, Father. . ."

Father de la Colombière smiled. "But why be afraid, Your Grace? Aren't we all in God's hands? All we have to do is to ask Him for strength and wisdom to bear this present trial properly."

"Y-yes. But Titus Oates has so many powerful friends in the government! And every one of them is only too anxious to believe all his lies! Why, it could well happen—"

"That there'll be martyrs in England? Yes, I agree with you."

"And you're not afraid, Father? You don't want to go back to France while there's still time?"

"YES, THERE'LL BE MARTYRS IN ENGLAND."

"No, Your Grace. I much prefer to remain where I am."

For a moment no further word was spoken as the beautiful young Duchess gazed in admiration at her spiritual director. What a saintly man God had sent to guide her soul! And what a hero! Certainly, despite his extreme pallor and recent loss of weight, few would suspect that he was seriously ill; or that he rarely experienced a good night's sleep, owing to his violent spells of coughing. Indeed, not once had a word of complaint escaped his lips since he had been stricken with tuberculosis some months ago. And yet, unless something was done for him very soon, he would surely not survive the chill dampness of another English winter. . .

Seemingly Father de la Colombière could read the Duchess' thoughts, and did not approve of them. "There, there, Your Grace, I'm not going to die yet," he said cheerfully. "After all, you know where true strength lies for everyone—man, woman or child."

The young Duchess managed a tremulous smile. "In. . .in the Sacred Heart, Father?"

"Yes. There is one treasure house that can never be emptied, no matter how often we draw upon it. So, do we long for wisdom, knowledge, peace, consolation, mercy, justice, love? They are all there, Your Grace. And all the other virtues, too. And just think! The more discouraged we are, the more depressed in our efforts to do God's Will, the more eager He is that we have recourse to all these treasures that await us in His Sacred Heart."

Slowly the Duchess felt her spirits begin to rise. "Oh, Father, what a wonderful place the world would be if only more people could understand about that!" she burst out. "But the way things are—"

Father de la Colombière nodded sympathetically. "Yes, the way things are, millions think of God only as a terrifying Being somewhere in the clouds. They never dream of loving Him, or of calling upon Him for help. Yet God wants us to fear only the loss of Him, not the possession."

With these and other words, Father de la Colombière soon succeeded in comforting the Duchess—to such an extent that when she finally left him, it was in a considerably happier frame of mind. Perhaps conditions for the Church in England were not as bad as they seemed, she told herself. Perhaps all the wild rantings of Titus Oates about a Catholic plot to murder King Charles the Second would soon be recognized for the stupid lies that they were and treated accordingly.

Alas for such hopes! By mid-October, the fiction of "The Popish Plot" had gained so many adherents that all England was seething with freshly kindled hatred of the Catholic Church. Scores of priests were rounded up and sent to prison. Edward Coleman, the Duchess' private secretary, was likewise arrested. Several Catholic peers were accused of treason and thrown into the Tower of London to stand trial for their lives. Then on the morning of November 24 came the dreadful news that Father de la Colombière had been seized. During the night an armed band of ruffians had broken into his quarters at Saint James Palace (the private residence of the Duke and Duchess of York), accused him of treason, and hauled him off to one of the filthiest prisons in the city. Despite the fact that recently he had suffered severe hemorrhages and was now so weak that he could scarcely walk, he was wanted for questioning.

Had he made converts to the Catholic Church while

serving as the Duchess' chaplain? Had he said Mass or administered the Sacraments in various private houses? Had he arranged for certain young men to escape to France and Italy to study for the priesthood? For certain young girls to be received there as religious? For other men and women to go to Maryland and Virginia, in the New World, to spread their dangerous Popish doctrines? If so, he was an enemy of the Crown and worthy of death. And a traitor's death at that.

CHAPTER 28

THE DUCHESS'
DESPERATE PLEA

A TRAITOR'S DEATH! Father de la Colombière was to be hanged, then drawn and quartered? That is, his body was to be taken down from the gallows while he was yet alive, ripped open with a sword and the insides pulled out, then hacked into four pieces and put on public display? Mary Beatrice was plunged into an agony of horror.

"James, it can't happen!" she told her husband frantically. "It *mustn't* happen! We'll have to do something right away. . ."

But what was to be done? The considerable political power which the Duke of York had once possessed had been taken from him five years before, after his conversion to the Church. As for King Charles the Second, he was most exasperatingly casual when the matter was broached to him.

"Calm yourself, my dear," he told his distraught young sister-in-law cheerfully. "There's nothing any of us can do now for Father de la Colombière. Just be grateful that the poor man doesn't mind being a martyr."

The Duchess' eyes flashed. "But that's scarcely the

point, Your Majesty. My chaplain's not a traitor. In fact, he's totally innocent of any crime."

"Of course, of course! And so are all the other unlucky wretches Titus Oates is sending to prison these days."

"*What?* Then you don't believe in the Popish Plot?"

King Charles threw back his head and laughed heartily. "Do you take me for a fool, Mary Beatrice? Why, Titus Oates is a lying, black-hearted scoundrel if I ever saw one!"

"But—"

"I've said it before and I say it again: his claim that the Catholics want to murder me and put your husband on the throne is sheer nonsense."

Mary Beatrice clasped her hands imploringly. "Then why don't you say so in public, Your Majesty? Why don't you do something about Father de la Colombière and all the other poor priests and laymen who've been so unjustly accused?"

The King shrugged. "Why should I?"

"But. . .but Your Majesty!"

"Ah, I'm wiser than you think, Mary Beatrice," observed the monarch, shaking a finger. "Almost thirty years ago my poor father made the mistake of going against public opinion when the people were wrought up. And you know what happened to him."

For a moment the young Duchess was silent. It was certainly true that when this aggravating brother-in-law had been but a boy of nineteen, his father, King Charles the First, had made himself so unpopular with the English people that they had risen up against him, established a Commonwealth under Oliver Cromwell and, on January 31, 1649, condemned their sovereign to the executioner's block. As a result, his two young sons,

Prince Charles and Prince James (the latter to be her husband one day), had been forced to live as exiles in France for eleven years. Only the death of Oliver Cromwell in 1658 and the subsequent failure of his son Richard to maintain an efficient government had made possible the return of Prince Charles to London in 1660, and the restoration of the present monarchy. Possibly, in view of such circumstances—

"Well, my dear, you seem to be having some weighty thoughts," said the King finally. "What is it that's troubling your pretty little head?"

Suddenly all the efforts of Mary Beatrice to be charitable and to exercise self-control were a failure. "You. . .you coward!" she stormed. "How can you joke at a time when innocent people are about to suffer a horrible death? Why can't you be brave enough to tell the truth? That Titus Oates is a villain, a vicious, scheming wretch of the worst sort—"

The King made a faint pretense of wiping away a tear. "Oh, my dear, I couldn't do that," he said regretfully. "Titus Oates is too popular a figure for me to oppose just now. Why, I'd run the risk of losing my throne if I even tried!"

"Risk! Who cares about risk? Father Claude de la Colombière is a priest of God, a saint! And if the least bit of harm comes to him, or to his fellow priests. . ."

King Charles gazed in amusement at the desperate young Duchess before him. "What a fine little speechmaker we have here!" he exclaimed jovially. "Go on, Mary Beatrice. I didn't think such a pious young woman could have so much fire in her."

"If it please Your Majesty—"

"Oh, don't stand on ceremony, my dear! Speak out plainly. What's going to happen if these Catholic friends

of yours swing by the neck? Is Hell going to swallow
me up because I permit England to have a few
martyrs?"

The continued lightheartedness of the English monarch was too much for Mary Beatrice. Suddenly, pale-
faced and tense, she burst into tears and rushed blindly
from the room. Dear God, what was going to happen?
Could nothing be done to save the saintly French Jesuit
who had been so kind to her? Who had come to
England, not through any wish of his own, but merely
out of obedience to his religious superiors?

"Perhaps the French King could be of help," the
Duke of York told his wife soothingly, when they were
alone. "Now, if we could get word to him in some
way. . ."

"But what could *he* do?" sobbed Mary Beatrice. "A
Frenchman and a Catholic himself, he wouldn't have
the slightest influence with Titus Oates or his bigoted
friends!"

"No, my dear. But he might have influence with
someone else."

"N-not King Charles!"

"Yes, King Charles. You see, despite what some people think, my brother is secretly anxious to keep on
good terms with Louis the Fourteenth. And if Louis
should point out that Father de la Colombière is a
French citizen; that he actually has the privileges of a
foreign diplomat because of being chaplain here at the
palace; that it's been a personal insult to have such a
man thrown into a common prison—"

A ray of hope dawned in Mary Beatrice's eyes.
"But. . .but the time's so short, James! Before we would
even get word to Paris. . ."

"Never mind about that. At least we can try."

So, very secretly, a letter was dispatched to the French capital and word of its going conveyed to Father de la Colombière. But the latter only smiled feebly when he heard the news. Heavy iron chains on wrists and ankles, his bed but a pile of verminous straw on the floor of a dingy cell, he had little hope of deliverance. And after all, what did freedom really matter now? He was so weak, so spent with coughing and hemorrhages, that his days on earth were surely numbered. "Thank the Duke and Duchess...for all that... they're trying...to do!" he stammered to the palace messenger, who had managed to bribe his way into the prison. "But also tell them...that I'm quite resigned ...to die!"

The messenger shivered. Could this pale, ragged creature lying at his feet, the prey of a dozen rats lurking in the shadows, actually be the celebrated French preacher who had spoken so eloquently about the Sacred Heart of Jesus just a few weeks ago? Why, he was more a corpse than a living man!

"Father, Her Grace the Duchess bids me tell you that if there is anything you would like—food, clothing, medicine..."

Father de la Colombière shook his head. "Thank you, no, I have all that I need." Then, after a moment: "Unless it could be arranged..."

"Yes, Father? What could we get you?"

"Pen, ink, paper. Time is getting so short now. It...it would never do to waste it..."

CHAPTER 29

THE INTERROGATION

PEN, INK, paper! The inmates of the other cells laughed uproariously when they heard about the request. What a fool the French Jesuit was! Why hadn't he asked for something worthwhile from his royal friends? Money, for instance. Moldy bread and stale water was the only fare served to prisoners, but if one had a few gold pieces it was easy enough to bribe the guards into getting a fair meal. Or even into removing the chains from one's wrists and ankles for an hour or so.

"What's the matter with you, priest?"

"Are you out of your mind?"

"It's too late now to be writing letters to the Pope!"

"You'll be dead before he even gets them!"

In the shadows Father de la Colombière tossed uneasily on his heap of straw. The air was foul in this damp and filthy hole, and the rats were a constant nightmare. But more distressing was the language of the other prisoners, the screams and curses of those dying from the dread typhus fever only a few yards away. Yet probably most of these poor people—the thieves, the drunkards, the murderers, the women, young and old, who had spent their lives in hideous sin—had been made children of God in the waters of Baptism. He must try to bring them back to repentance, to Sanctifying Grace...

"Sacred Heart of Jesus, have mercy on them!" Father de la Colombière prayed. "Father, forgive them, for they know not what they do—"

Occasionally sleep came to the Jesuit, so that he forgot his surroundings. Once again he was back in France, in Paray-le-Monial, listening to the pleading voice of a humble young nun. Our Lord wished for souls, she said, generous souls who were not afraid to make reparation for sinners. He must search out these faithful servants and tell them of the great power for good in devotion to the Sacred Heart; of the marvels of grace that could be won through the weekly Holy Hour and the reception of Holy Communion on First Fridays.

I will establish peace in their families.

I will console them in all their difficulties.

I will be their assured refuge in life, and more especially at death...

Then, when two days had passed...

"All right, Jesuit, you're wanted this morning for questioning," a guard announced tersely. "On your feet, man. It won't do to keep the Marquis of Winchester waiting. Or His Lordship either."

Father de la Colombière, freed from the iron fetters, struggled painfully to his feet. "His Lordship, you say?"

"Yes, stupid, His Lordship. The Most Reverend Titus Oates, Doctor of Divinity from the University of Salamanca."

A faint smile flickered on the priest's lips. So, the Catholics' arch-enemy had suddenly taken to himself a Bishop's rank in the heretical Church of England. Also that of a scholar from Spain's leading university, although it was common knowledge that he had never even been in Salamanca.

"Very well. I'm ready," he said quietly.

The trip to court was a quick one, and soon Father de la Colombière was trying to hold himself erect before the Marquis of Winchester, presiding magistrate, in a narrow room packed with jeering men and women. The atmosphere was tense.

"Ugh, there's the French Jesuit!"

"The Pope's own spy!"

"Look at the guilty face on him!"

"Ha, he thought he could get away with murdering the King!"

"Then put James on the throne!"

"No, no! Death to the traitor!"

"Away with the wretch!"

"Hang the stupid fool!"

"Yes, hang him! Hang him!"

Pompous and overbearing in his wig and robes of office, the Marquis of Winchester rapped sharply for order. What was the prisoner's name, age, occupation? Did he know that he must truthfully answer these and all other questions put to him?

Calm and unafraid, Father de la Colombière quietly gave the desired information. Then suddenly a side door opened and thunderous applause swept through the crowded courtroom. Titus Oates, in imposing epis-copal attire, accompanied by a shifty-faced layman, one William Bedloe, had arrived to question the prisoner!

The Jesuit gazed in dismay as his chief accuser swag-gered forward. Why, this man's appearance was posi-tively hideous! Surely it wasn't possible that such a person had won the support of thousands in England?

"Ha, priest, so we've caught up with you at last!" said Oates, rubbing his hands with satisfaction. "Well, it's about time. Come, now—only the truth. When did you plan to kill the King?"

Father de la Colombière, seized by a sudden coughing spell, barely managed to keep erect. "I . . .I am innocent of any such crime!" he gasped. "And so are all my brother priests. . ."

"Liar! His Majesty was to have died before Christmas!"

"No, no, I tell you. . ."

"And with what delicacy! By silver bullets, no less, out of respect for his rank!"

A storm of jeers and catcalls rang through the courtroom, and it was some minutes before order could be restored. Then Oates resumed his questioning. Hadn't Father de la Colombière made several converts to the Catholic Church while serving as private chaplain to the Duchess of York? Hadn't he frequently boasted, in word and in letters to France, of the progress he was making in furthering the Pope's cause? And wasn't he being well paid for his efforts from the Pope's own treasury? Now, who were those traitors who had aided and abetted him?

Calmly Father de la Colombière admitted that the two years he had spent in England had been devoted to helping people to know God better, to love and serve Him. If this was a crime, so be it. But he was no paid enemy of the Crown. He had never wished His Majesty ill, or plotted his death. As for giving the names of any converts he was supposed to have made—

"I have nothing to say about that," he declared quietly.

In vain Titus Oates fumed and ranted, likewise his friend William Bedloe and a certain Oliver Fiquet who had been brought in as a witness against the accused.

"WHEN DID YOU PLAN TO KILL THE KING?"

Repeatedly Father de la Colombière denied all their charges concerning the existence of a Popish Plot, and any treachery on his own part. However, such constancy did not please the crowd, and there was a steady chorus of jeers, threats and curses.

"Death to the liar!"

"Hang the priest!"

"Away with the Pope's tool!"

Finally the Marquis of Winchester issued a decision. Everyone knew there was a Popish Plot, he said. Only a fool would argue that point. Perhaps this priest might not have had any actual part in it, but the mere fact that he did not deny having made converts to the Catholic Church was sufficient reason for him to go to trial for his life before the Lord Chief Justice.

"Guards, return the accused to prison!" he snapped. Then, shaking a warning finger: "And watch him well. There's no doubt he's a sly fellow, with many a trick up his sleeve."

CHAPTER 30

FRANCE AGAIN

THE DREARY month of November gave place to December, with its ever-increasing dampness and cold. Racked with pain, fever and continual coughing, Father de la Colombière nevertheless tried constantly to keep in mind that the future was entirely in God's hands. Repeatedly from his bed of straw he offered himself as a victim for sinners, entreating the grace to die bravely when the time should come. For surely, following his appearance before the Lord Chief Justice, it would be his lot to be hanged, drawn and quartered? Already six men, including Edward Coleman, the Duchess of York's private secretary, and Father Mico, a Jesuit priest, had suffered this dreadful fate for their alleged connection with the so-called Popish Plot. And the word was that many more executions were to follow.

Then, wonder of wonders! On December 21 Father de la Colombière was roused from a fitful sleep by a violent commotion at the door of his cell. The rattle of keys, the creaking of rusty iron hinges, the grunts and curses of guards stumbling about in the shadows, and suddenly the galling chains were being removed from his wrists and ankles and he was being dragged to his feet!

"All right, priest!" bellowed a voice somewhere in the distance. "Come on! You're a free man now."

There were kindlier voices, too—trembling, excited, urgent. "It's the truth, Father! You don't have to stand trial after all!"

"The Duke and Duchess have arranged your release!"

"There's nothing more to worry about!"

"You're even going back to France!"

"But don't try to ask questions."

"No, just come with us."

"We've a carriage waiting outside."

More dead than alive, the Jesuit did not fully realize what was happening. But once he had arrived at his familiar quarters in Saint James Palace, his mind cleared and he set about to learn the details of his release. Thus, a few days before, King Louis the Fourteenth had protested so vigorously against the imprisonment of one of his loyal subjects that the English authorities had been impressed in spite of themselves. Now the charges against him were being dropped. Instead of having to stand trial, he was being expelled from the country and sent back to his native France.

"But you don't have to go right away, Father," announced the Duchess of York consolingly. "You're to have a ten-day rest here with us, so as to gain back enough strength to make the trip safely."

The ten days of rest and loving care passed with the speed of lightning. But long before December 31, when it was time to set out from London for Dover (where a ship was waiting to take him back to France), Father de la Colombière knew that he could never repay his many English friends for all their kindness. All he could do was to keep them in his prayers, especially the Duke

and Duchess, and to beg of God that soon the terrible
days of religious persecution would be over. As for those
who had already given their lives as martyrs, and who
still might be called upon to do so—

"Sacred Heart of Jesus, have mercy on them!" he
begged. "Be their consolation and reward . . ."

The Jesuits in Paris, when they heard the first-hand
account of all the dreadful things which had been happening to their fellow religious, also joined in prayer for
the suffering brethren in England. And of course they
could not do enough for Father de la Colombière himself. Plenty of rest, good food and medical care were
the order of the day. However, when two months had
passed, it was decided that a change of air would probably do the invalid more good than anything. Winter in
Paris was extremely trying for anyone with lung trouble.
Wouldn't it be far better if Father de la Colombière
should go south to Lyons for a while, stopping at Dijon
and Paray-le-Monial to break the hardship of the
journey?

Paray-le-Monial! Father de la Colombière's heart beat
fast when, late in March, 1679, he finally arrived in the
sleepy little town. What an eternity since he had set
out from here on his secret mission to England! And
yet it was only two and one-half years, years that might
be considered lost save for the fact that in them he had
managed to spread a fervent devotion to the Sacred
Heart among hundreds of English Catholics. Even now
countless numbers of these chosen souls were risking
their lives in order to receive Holy Communion on the
First Fridays. They were keeping a Holy Hour each
Thursday night, too, and making generous reparation for
sinners. What though his original task—the conversion
of King Charles the Second—had not been accom-

plished? Perhaps what had been done would be of more use to the Church in the long run than anything else.

Yet even as he tried to find consolation in such a hope, Father de la Colombière's thoughts kept turning to Sister Margaret Mary. In just a little while, he told himself, in the convent parlor, she would be describing to him all the blessings which Our Lord surely must have showered upon her during the last two and one-half years. True, she had occasionally mentioned some of these in her letters, especially when Mother de Saumaise had been superior. But how much more satisfying to hear from her own lips of new messages from Heaven.

However, the eighty-mile trip from Dijon (where he had had the great satisfaction of visiting with Mother de Saumaise herself) proved to be far too much for Father de la Colombière. For two days he was forced to rest at the Jesuit college before being able to present himself at the Visitation monastery. Then, what a shock to learn that the new superior, Mother Greyfié, was not in favor of his having an immediate visit with Sister Margaret Mary! Instead, she had arranged for him to address the community, all of whom were desperately eager to hear about his adventures in England. Also, a number of Sisters wished to go to confession. Perhaps, after his talk, he would be good enough to accommodate them?

Father de la Colombière managed to smile cheerfully. Another little cross to bear for sinners? Well, so be it. He would have his private visit with Sister Margaret Mary when confessions were over. But at this, Mother Greyfié shook her head, politely but firmly.

"No, Father. I'm sorry, but you can't see Sister Margaret Mary today or any other day. She doesn't deserve such a privilege."

The Jesuit stared in amazement. "But surely you're not serious, Mother!"

The superior's lips tightened. "Yes, Father. Quite serious."

"But I don't understand! What possible reason—"

"Just this, Father. Sister Margaret Mary causes me more trouble than anyone else in the community. Now, no matter what the cost, she must be taught a proper respect for authority; to keep her place, and not to be running after people with fantastic talk about heavenly visions and voices." Then, after a moment: "Of course, if she wishes to speak with you in the confessional, that is an entirely different matter. I can scarcely forbid that."

The priest felt his heart sink. So, like the other superiors before her, Mother Greyfié was having trouble realizing that his spiritual daughter was one of God's chosen souls? And this, after nearly a year's residence in Paray-le-Monial? How poor Sister Margaret Mary must be suffering!

"Very well, Mother," he said quietly. "Just as you wish."

CHAPTER 31

THINGS START TO CLEAR UP

SOON, the hardships of recent months became as nothing to Sister Margaret Mary. And as she made known to Father de la Colombière the many remarkable graces she had received from Our Lord, the priest's own heart filled with a rare and consoling peace. How good to be given another glimpse into the soul of a saint! To see how inwardly beautiful a poor human creature can become once it has abandoned itself completely to God's Will!

And yet—

"Sister, why not tell me about Mother Greyfié?" he suggested suddenly. "Is she helping to promote devotion to the Sacred Heart?"

There was a moment's silence. Then Sister Margaret Mary spoke—slowly, reluctantly. "Father, if you don't mind—"

The Jesuit leaned forward intently. "Ah, but I *do* mind! Mother Greyfié has been making you suffer, hasn't she? And for no apparent reason?"

Again there was silence. But little by little, with much prompting from Father de la Colombière, the unfortunate story began to unfold. Mother Greyfié was a most devout religious, but also of an exceedingly practical turn of mind. Ever since her arrival at the monastery, ten months ago, she had been unable to accept the truth about Our Lord's apparitions. They were the work of the Devil, she insisted, the fruit of pride and stubbornness. In fact, for a time she had even gone so far as to forbid Sister Margaret Mary to make her weekly Holy Hour. However, following the sudden death last October 14 of Sister Mary Elizabeth Quarré (a young religious to whom she was most devoted), she had somewhat fearfully restored the privilege. Yet she was still convinced that only severity and harsh words could loosen the Devil's grip on Sister Margaret Mary's soul and bring her to her senses.

"But I love her just the same, Father," commented Sister Margaret Mary simply. "And some day I'm sure the grace will come, and Mother will do all in her power to promote devotion to the Sacred Heart. In the meantime, God couldn't have sent us a better superior. I've learned *so* much from her! So very much!"

Father de la Colombière did not argue the point.

But soon afterward it happened that Mother Greyfié subjected Sister Margaret Mary to additional humiliation at the next community chapter meeting—by calling attention disapprovingly to her long conference with Father de la Colombière.

Before he returned to the Jesuit college, the priest had a heart-to-heart talk with Mother Greyfié. Didn't she realize what a grave mistake it was to be so harsh with Sister Margaret Mary? This thirty-two-year-old religious was not out of her mind, or in the Devil's power. She was a saint of God, and some day Paray-le-Monial would be famous because of her.

Sister Margaret Mary did not at all act like a person who was being deceived by the Devil. Rather, she was

always humble, perfectly obedient, simple and morti-
fied. These were good signs of God's work, not of the
Devil's.

Indeed, so forceful were the priest's words that soon
Mother Greyfié was on the point of tears.

"But I meant no harm, Father!" she burst out. "It's
just that. . .well, I didn't know whether these visions
were really from God. And then, the Visitation Order
has never been an order to encourage these extraordinary spiritual ways. . ."

"Just remember this, Mother," the priest continued
bluntly. "God's ways are not always our ways. Many
times He chooses the poor, the sick, the uneducated,
to do some of His most important work. And when He
does, not one of us should dare to question why."

"No, Father, of course not," admitted Mother Greyfié
hastily. "I understand that quite well." And indeed,
Mother Greyfié did feel strongly reassured about Sister
Margaret Mary since listening to Father de la
Colombière's words.

But would things really be better now, Father de la
Colombière asked himself, as he made his way back to
the Jesuit college in Paray-le-Monial. Without intending
any harm, the zealous superior could still be the cause
of much suffering for Sister Margaret Mary by the
abruptness of her ways and the sharpness of her tongue.

"Dear Lord, please give me some of Sister Margaret
Mary's patience!" he pleaded silently.

There was frequent need to repeat this prayer, especially in the long weeks of convalescence that he spent
at the Jesuit house in Lyons. What a cross to be an
invalid! To be constantly weak and tired, and of no use
to anyone!

Yet even as the depressing thoughts came, Father de

la Colombière firmly set them aside. His present state
of poor health was what God had chosen for him. For
the time being, it was the only key which would open
that particular door to Heaven through which he was
meant to enter. How foolish, then, to want to throw it
away! To regret the fact that he had not been found worthy to suffer martyrdom with his fellow priests in
England, several of whom had died on the gallows since
his own return to France. . .

Ah, yes, God knew best, as He always did. The soul's
task was to abandon itself to Him, trusting in Him
completely.

By mid-October Father de la Colombière's health was
better. So much better, in fact, that the superiors
decided to give him a little work. He was to be spiritual
director for the young men who were studying for the
priesthood in the Society of Jesus at Lyons. He would
also be confessor for the youngest boys at the college.

From the start, Father de la Colombière endeared
himself to all his student charges. He made friends, too,
with various laymen in the city. There was just one trouble with the good priest, these gentlemen told one
another reluctantly. He was forever urging a devotion
to the Sacred Heart of Jesus, picturing Our Lord as a
Man of Sorrows seeking reparation and consolation.
Well, this type of prayer might appeal to pious nuns in
their cloister, or even to certain sentimental women in
the world, but surely it was never intended for men?

Father de la Colombière was neither shocked nor
alarmed by such an attitude. "Actually, my friends, sen-
timentalism has nothing to do with the devotion," he
replied cheerfully. "It's a matter of love—and we know
that love is something strong, sometimes something
hard."

"ISN'T THE SACRED HEART DEVOTION
JUST FOR SENTIMENTAL WOMEN, FATHER?"

The men were listening. The priest went on.

"When Our Lord asked the three favored Apostles— Peter, James and John—to watch and pray with Him in the Garden of Gethsemane, He was asking them to do something difficult for love of Him. They had the chance to share His sorrow, to help console Him. Our Lord chose three men for this task."

"That's true," replied one of the men thoughtfully.

"But we know they failed Him," continued Father de la Colombière. "If their love had been stronger, they would not have failed. As for ourselves, however, by devotion to Our Lord's Sacred Heart, we somehow have a share in consoling Him in the Garden of Gethsemane."

"We do?"

"Yes. Furthermore, we help make up for and console Our Lord for the terrible offenses that are committed against Him every day, and for people's coldness and ingratitude. We know how painful it is when someone we have been very good to is not thankful. Now, if we think about all Our Lord has done for us, we will want to return His love, especially when we think of how our sins have made Him suffer."

"Yes, I can understand that, Father."

"Plus, we win graces to convert souls from sin so they can be with Our Lord for all eternity, instead of cursing Him forever in Hell."

"That makes sense too, Father. But why all this emphasis on suffering and sorrow?"

"Suffering and sorrow entered the world as the result of sin," replied Father de la Colombière. "However, there is now a very good use to be made of them. Many people don't know it, but suffering is closely related to love."

"Hmm," mumbled one of the men, as he continued

to listen.

"Suffering can express love," continued the priest, "and it is a powerful means to make love grow. Remember that on the Cross Our Lord said, 'I thirst.' He meant mainly a thirst for souls and for our love. Our Lord's sufferings were terribly powerful at that moment—but His love for us was even more powerful. The saints choose suffering because they have a fire of love for Our Lord in their souls. That divine love comes from Sanctifying Grace. It burns up their weakness and their cowardice. Think of St. Paul, St. Francis Xavier, the martyrs...By comparison, most of us give Him back a love that is weak and lukewarm."

"I guess I'm not a saint yet, Father," commented one of the men with a sheepish smile.

"Love grows by loving," responded Father de la Colombière quickly. "If you have Sanctifying Grace in your soul, you already have at least a little love for Our Lord. That's a good start. The next thing is to try to understand about Our Lord's love and suffering, and to offer Him some acts of love and reparation. And the rewards you receive from Him will be all out of proportion to the efforts you give Him."

For a moment the men were silent, carried out of themselves by this fresh vision. Then presently, a bit timid and embarrassed, they asked their final questions. What was the best way of loving God and of making reparation for offenses against Him? Of persuading friends and neighbors to do likewise?

The answer was very simple, said Father de la Colombière. It was to assist at Mass—that glorious renewal of the great Sacrifice of Calvary—and to receive Holy Communion. This was the most perfect prayer of love and reparation which man could offer to God. Long ago the Devil had discovered the value of this secret weapon, and found himself absolutely powerless against it. But being an angel with an angel's superior intelligence (despite his fallen state), he was busily sowing tricky lies, spreading the heresy that man should not speak to God as to a loving Father or receive Him in Holy Communion. If Christians must do such things, once or twice a year would suffice. But as for making the practice so frequent as to include the First Friday of every month...

"Ah, my friends, the mere thought of that has been just too much for the Devil!" declared the Jesuit earnestly. "Now there's nothing he won't do to make such a devotion unpopular, misunderstood, even ridiculed for being extreme. And so far, alas, he's had fair success."

The men looked at each other in dismay. So it was the Devil who had been making them suspicious of devotion to the Sacred Heart of Jesus? Who had caused them not to appreciate the importance of a monthly Communion of reparation? To believe that a weekly Holy Hour was a form of piety suited only to cloistered nuns and pious women in the world? Well, no more. From now on they would do all in their power to foster these practices in their own lives, and in the lives of friends and neighbors.

"It's a man's work after all, Father, not just something for women and girls!"

"Why, it's almost like being an apostle! And the apostles were certainly real men—even heroes."

The Jesuit smiled. "It *is* being an apostle," he said quietly. "The very best kind."

But when the two had finally taken their departure, grateful beyond words for Father de la Colombière's helpful comments and filled with zeal for their new-found apostolate, a faint smile flickered on the Jesuit's lips. His friends were good men, of course, sincere and well-meaning, but how long would their present enthusiasm endure? The Devil was no fool. As the days passed, he would surely do his utmost to spoil their efforts. In his hands criticism, ridicule, physical fatigue, even indifference, were powerful weapons. Eventually they could so weaken the will as to make failures of the most zealous of workers. On the other hand, if these friends could be induced to put their confidence in the Heart of Jesus instead of in themselves. . . to commend themselves to Him several times a day. . .

"There'd be far less chance of failure then," Father de la Colombière reflected. "I must remind them about that as soon as I can. And I mustn't forget to ask Sister Margaret Mary to pray for them, too."

Naturally Sister Margaret Mary was only too glad to help the new friends of her spiritual director, and to continue her prayers for him as well. Indeed, for a while it seemed as though God had heard these prayers. Apparently the dreaded tuberculosis had been checked, and there was a chance for complete recovery. But at Easter, 1681, after he had been working in Lyons for some eighteen months, the Jesuit superiors were forced to admit that Father de la Colombière could not survive another winter in the city. His only hope for better health lay in being transferred to some country town, possibly Paray-le-Monial, where the climate was milder and there would be no long lines of students and other visitors waiting to see him.

Paray-le-Monial! When Father de la Colombière arrived there in August of 1681, he was well-nigh exhausted. And discouraged, too, at the thought of being a burden to others of his fellow Jesuits. If only he could have brought more souls to the Sacred Heart during his lifetime of forty years! If only he could have prayed and suffered with greater charity! If only he could have died a martyr in the persecution connected with "The Popish Plot," as the holy Archbishop of Armagh, Oliver Plunket, had done just a month ago! But this way—

"Ah, but this way is God's way," whispered the loyal voice of conscience. "Just wait and see."

At Father de la Colombière's next meeting with Sister Margaret Mary (arranged this time with no opposition from Mother Greyfié), Sister Margaret Mary agreed. In fact, Our Lord had told her that if Father de la Colombière were well, he would glorify Him by his zeal, but since he was ill, Our Lord would glorify *Himself* in Father de la Colombière.

Yes, Father de la Colombière's active life might be over, but he still could be of use to others by patiently bearing the heavy cross of illness. And who was to say that a childlike trust in God's Providence might not win more grace than giving a course of eloquent sermons? Than writing many spiritual books? Than martyrdom itself?

Yes, thought Father de la Colombière: sickness was a cross, but it was a grace, too. It could be very good for the soul. It was one of God's tools for breaking off one's last little attachments to self-will—attachments that one didn't even see!

Ah, yes, he could see that sickness had been a great grace.

CHAPTER 32

MYSTERIOUS MESSAGES

A S THE weeks passed, the Jesuits in Paray-le-Monial were forced to the sad realization that their beloved Father de la Colombière would not be with them much longer. True, on December 3, the feast of Saint Francis Xavier, he had managed to offer the Holy Sacrifice and to receive a few visitors. But by January, 1682, his health had declined to the point where he could no longer feed or dress himself, much less leave his bed. Nevertheless, it was decided that the invigorating air of Vienne (a town some seventy-five miles to the southeast) might benefit the invalid, especially as his younger brother Floris was a priest there and would see that he had every attention. So a comfortable carriage was procured, and arrangements made to begin the journey on January 29, the feast of Saint Francis de Sales.

It was Catherine de Bisfranc, a devoted spiritual daughter of the Jesuit, who first brought the unexpected news to Sister Margaret Mary.

"Everything's all settled!" she exclaimed tearfully. "Father Floris is on his way here now! Oh, Sister! In just a few hours, unless there's a miracle of some sort, they'll be taking Father de la Colombière away for good..."

For a moment Sister Margaret Mary looked startled. Then she shook her head. "No, that mustn't happen," she said quietly. "Catherine, go at once to the Jesuit superior and tell him that Father de la Colombière must not leave for Vienne, if this is possible without any disobedience."

Catherine gasped. "But Sister—"

"Quickly, there's no time to lose."

Dabbing at her reddened eyes, Catherine hurried off to the Jesuit house (which was only a few doors from the convent) and delivered the startling message to Father Bourguignet, the superior.

"But the superiors in Lyons have already arranged details," protested the latter. "Besides, Father de la Colombière wants to go with his brother."

However, after a hurried trip to the sickroom, Father Bourguignet returned with the word that Father de la Colombière wanted to know the reason for Sister Margaret Mary's message. Could she send him a little note of explanation?

Within just a few minutes a much happier Catherine was back at the Jesuit house with a scrap of paper bearing two hastily scribbled lines: "He has told me that He wishes the sacrifice of your life here."

Father Bourguignet stared in amazement. What was to be done now? Sister Margaret Mary was a saint, of course, and seemingly Our Lord had given her this unusual message. But what about the orders from the superiors in Lyons? Would they agree to this change of plans? And what about Father Floris da la Colombière, just arrived, who had been so eagerly looking forward to having his brother under his own roof until God should take him?

"Mademoiselle, I'll have to think about all this," he

CATHERINE WAS MUCH HAPPIER NOW.

told Catherine reluctantly. "It's. . .well, it's a little too much for me to figure out just now."

When informed of the excitement her words had caused, Sister Margaret Mary did not seem at all surprised. Nor was she surprised at the message which eventually arrived from Father de la Colombière himself, after some delay. Since a religious ought to be "like a corpse in the hands of the washers of the dead," he declared, quoting the famous words of Saint Ignatius, he was obeying the orders of the superiors in Lyons and setting out for Vienne as soon as possible.

Catherine de Bisfranc, greatly depressed, found little consolation in Sister Margaret Mary's repeated assurance that all would be well, their good friend would die in Paray-le-Monial and be buried there, too.

"No, no!" she sobbed. "He's going to be taken from us! I *know* it!"

But on the day before the scheduled departure, Father de la Colombière was suddenly stricken with a fever so severe that he could not possibly be moved. For a week he hovered on the brink of eternity, while his friends stormed Heaven on his behalf. Then, at seven o'clock in the evening of February 15, thirteen days after his forty-first birthday, death came at last.

Sister Margaret Mary was surprisingly calm when she heard the news. "Pray for him, and get others to pray, too," she urged the weeping Catherine when the latter arrived at the monastery at five o'clock in the morning of the next day. However, at ten o'clock, during the funeral service, there was a more consoling message, which she committed to paper for her friend.

"Stop worrying. Invoke him. Fear nothing. He has more power now to help you than ever before."

Mother Greyfié scarcely knew what to think when

she considered the contrast in the two messages. Surely it couldn't be possible that Father de la Colombière had had to spend even a little while in Purgatory?

"Sister, this is preposterous!" she burst out. "Why, our good Father was a wonderfully holy man!"

Sister Margaret Mary nodded calmly. "Yes, Mother. But in order to satisfy for some negligences in the exercise of divine love, his soul was deprived of the sight of God from the moment of death until his body was laid to rest in the grave."

Mother Greyfié shuddered. Suddenly it seemed as though she had never really known Sister Margaret Mary until now. How resigned she was! How completely absorbed in doing God's Will! Could it be possible that many of the most important members of the community had been misjudging this thirty-five-year-old religious ever since her arrival at the monastery eleven years before? That Our Lord really did appear to her from time to time? That the request for a Communion of reparation on the First Fridays was not the product of a sick brain, or of a stubborn human will, but the glorious truth itself? If so, what dreadful negligence she, Mother Greyfié, would have to atone for someday!

"Sister, I don't know what to say!" she blurted out finally.

"Ah, there's no need to say anything, Mother," replied Sister Margaret Mary sweetly. "Father de la Colombière is in Heaven now, praying for both of us. That's all that really matters."

Yet, after the emotional excitement occasioned by Father de la Colombière's death had spent itself, Mother Greyfié was assaulted by fresh misgivings with regard to Sister Margaret Mary. On December 21, 1682, ten months later, she suddenly made up her mind to settle the case of Sister Margaret Mary once and for all. For some time the nun had been seriously ill in the infirmary. Well, if Our Lord would immediately grant her perfect health, and let it continue for the next five months, she, Mother Greyfié, would have no more doubts concerning the so-called apparitions. In fact, she would do all in her power to promote a general devotion to the Sacred Heart of Jesus.

"See? I've put all this in writing," she told Sister Margaret Mary abruptly. "Now, in the name of holy obedience, Sister, get out of bed, take this paper to the chapel, and tell Our Lord that I'm waiting for an answer. An once, do you hear? We're about to have Benediction."

Sister Margaret Mary, weak though she was, managed a faint smile. "Yes, Mother," she whispered. "At once."

CHAPTER 33

THREE MORE PROMISES

WITHIN THE hour Mother Greyfié received her answer. At the elevation of the monstrance during Benediction, Sister Margaret Mary knew that Our Lord had granted her request. She would have perfect health for the next five months—or until May 21, 1683.

"Well, we'll see," said the superior dryly when she heard the news.

Yet deep within herself, even as she spoke, she felt her former prejudices beginning to crumble. Indeed, as winter gave place to spring and Sister Margaret Mary continued to enjoy the best of health, Mother Greyfié suffered agonies of remorse. What a fool she had been to have entertained any doubts as to the sanctity of this religious! Why, God Himself had proved that, over and over again, but she had always been too blind to assent to His proof.

However, on May 21, Mother Greyfié did feel impelled to ask for one more favor. Would Sister Margaret Mary beg the Heavenly Father to let her enjoy her present good health for the balance of the year? After that, He might do with her as He wished.

Once again the superior's request was granted, and

the following May, when her six-year term of office was at an end and she was preparing to leave for Semur, she broke down completely.

"Sister, how can you ever forgive my lack of understanding?" she burst out. "Oh, when I think of the many times I've been unkind to you...even cruel...."

The sight of Mother Greyfié in tears was too much for Sister Margaret Mary. "Mother, please don't say that!" she begged. "Don't you know that Our Lord permitted everything? That He *wanted* me to suffer—for a special reason?"

A special reason! Well did the older religious realize what this was. And as she pressed Sister Margaret Mary to her in fond farewell, she made a solemn promise. At the Visitation monastery in Semur, where she would be serving as superior, she would do all in her power to promote devotion to the Sacred Heart. She would receive Holy Communion on the First Friday of each month, make a Holy Hour every Thursday night, and do her best to explain to the Sisters the real meaning of reparation, so that they also would be eager to make these practices their own.

Certain members of the community at Paray-le-Monial were secretly displeased when they heard about all this. And when it became known that their new superior, Mother Mary Christine Melin, had arranged for Sister Margaret Mary to be raised to the important post of First Assistant, then to become Novice Mistress, they could no longer hide their true feelings. Why, as Novice Mistress, Sister Margaret Mary would have complete charge of the youngest members of the community! She it would be, more than anyone else, who would watch over their spiritual development and explain to them the Holy Rule!

"That's certainly a mistake!" exclaimed Sister Magdalen des Escures irritably.

Sister Antoinette de Coligny sighed and shook her head. "I just don't know," she muttered. "Certainly from now on the poor novices are going to be utterly misled. Mark my words."

"Yes," agreed Sister Claudia d'Amanze. "There'll be nothing else for them but talks on this new-fangled devotion to the Sacred Heart."

"Not a word about the writings of Saint Francis de Sales, or of Mother de Chantal."

"Of course not. And you know what that means."

"Complete ignorance of the spirit of the Order?"

"Worse than that. It will spell the ruin of the whole monastery!"

But Mother Melin only smiled when such remarks reached her ears. "I've known Sister Margaret Mary for a long time," she said calmly. "I have every confidence in her."

The majority of the Sisters agreed with Mother Melin that she had made a wise choice, including the five novices themselves: Sister Frances Rosalie Verchère, Sister Péronne Margaret Verchère, Sister Péronne Rosalie de Farges, Sister Mary Frances Bocaud and Sister Mary Christine Bouthier. Ever since they had come to the monastery they had been admiring their prospective Mistress from afar, and marveling at the many exciting stories about her. For instance, didn't the Souls in Purgatory often come to ask her prayers for a speedy release from suffering? Hadn't several people, even in distant places, experienced miracles through her intercession? Then, Our Lord Himself! Hadn't He appeared to her dozens of times, and made all manner of thrilling promises in favor of those who should practice devotion to His Sacred Heart or promote devotion to It?

"Eight promises," announced Sister Frances Rosalie solemnly.

But Sister Mary Christine, the latest arrival in the novitiate, shook her head doubtfully. "In town they've been saying there are ten promises," she declared. "At least, that's what a good friend told my mother."

Ten promises! The novices looked at one another in wide-eyed astonishment. What could the two other promises be? Perhaps Mother Margaret Mary (for that was her title now) wouldn't mind telling them?

The new Mistress of Novices was more than willing to satisfy the curiosity of her young charges. Yes, Our Lord had made many wonderful promises. Eleven promises, if one wanted to be exact.

"*Eleven*, Mother!" exclaimed Sister Frances Rosalie. "But I thought there were only eight! Please, what are the other three?"

Mother Margaret Mary smiled fondly at the eager young faces raised to hers. What joy to be living in the novitiate! To have such an important part to play in leading these innocent souls to perfection!

"The three new promises, children? You really want to know about them?"

"Oh, yes, Mother! Please!"

For a moment Mother Margaret Mary was silent, while a faraway look crept into her dark eyes. Then, folding her hands as though in prayer, she began to speak:

"I will bless the houses in which the image of My Sacred Heart shall be exposed and honored. I will give to priests the power of moving the most hardened hearts. Persons who propagate this devotion shall have their names inscribed in My Heart, and they shall never be effaced from It."

The novices gazed at their Mistress in awed silence. Suddenly it seemed as though they were being given a glimpse into Heaven, and that it was Our Lord Himself who was speaking! However, apparently reading their thoughts, Mother Margaret Mary hastily came to herself and broke the spell. According to the Holy Rule, she reminded them gently, there was work to be done now. And prayers to be said, too. They would talk about Our Lord's promises some other time.

The senior novice, Sister Frances Rosalie, rose promptly to her feet. Like Sister Anne Rosselin before her, she had suddenly been struck by the exciting thought that some day Our Lord would make an even more important promise to Mother Margaret Mary— something so marvelous in its scope as to defy all imagining. What a pity that there was no time now to discuss such an idea! But as the Novice Mistress had pointed out, there was work to be done. And prayers to offer.

"Yes, Mother," she said cheerfully, making a valiant effort to remember the value of obedience. "We're coming."

CHAPTER 34

OUR LORD CLAIMS A VICTIM

A FEW WEEKS later, in mid-February, 1685, there was great excitement among the Jesuits in Paray-le-Monial. Word had just arrived that in faraway England, on February 6, death had come to King Charles the Second. And wonder of wonders! The fifty-five-year-old monarch, who had spent so much of his life in sinful luxury, who had been too fearful of personal consequences to take a public stand against the Popish Plot and thus save many of his loyal subjects from the gallows, had been received into the Catholic Church before his death!

"The prayers of Father de la Colombière were surely responsible for all this," one priest told another. "Why, it's nothing short of a miracle!"

The Jesuits in Paris and in Lyons were in total agreement. Nevertheless, they also realized that it would be a long time before their English Catholic brethren could enjoy true freedom. Now, although the Duke of York had succeeded to the throne and was reigning as King James the Second, although twenty-seven-year-old Mary Beatrice was a devout and worthy helpmate, a deep hatred of everything Catholic still persisted throughout the country. And this, despite the fact that

long ago Titus Oates had been proved a liar and been
sentenced to life imprisonment for his crimes against
the innocent.

"The new King and Queen are certainly to be pitied,"
was the general opinion. "So many people have the mistaken idea that they're going to force everyone to
become a Catholic, then hand the whole country over
to the Pope."

"But that's ridiculous!"

"Of course. But with so much lying gossip in circula-
tion, who's to believe that?"

However, as the weeks passed, there began to be
fresh hope that Father de la Colombière would watch
over his friends in England and secure for King James
the Second a peaceful and prosperous reign. Also, that
he would soon win the great blessing of a son and heir
for the English monarch. After all, one had only to read
the newly-published book of the sermons he had
preached while serving as the Queen's private chaplain
to realize what a holy man he had been. Surely he was
a saint in Heaven now, with even greater power before
the throne of God?

Back in Paray-le-Monial, the novices in the Visitation
convent were busy with another matter. As summer
drew near, their big concern was how they were going
to celebrate the feast of Saint Margaret of Antioch, the
patroness of their beloved Novice Mistress, on July 20.
Truly this day ought to have something very special
about it. And, if possible, their little celebration also
ought to be connected in some way with devotion to
the Sacred Heart.

"But how are we going to arrange that?" demanded
Sister Péronne Rosalie anxiously.

How, indeed! For days the novices racked their brains

for ideas. Then finally Sister Frances Rosalie came forward with a suggestion. A month ago, on the Friday after the octave of Corpus Christi, Mother Margaret Mary had set up a crude pen-and-ink sketch of the Sacred Heart on a small altar in the novitiate. Well, suppose they were to take this same drawing and make it the center of an attractive shrine? In other words, a real altar in honor of the Sacred Heart?

"With candles and flowers and ferns, like we had in the chapel for Corpus Christi?" asked Sister Péronne Margaret hopefully.

"With candles and flowers and ferns," replied Sister Frances Rosalie serenely. "After all, I'm sure that would please our Mother more than anything else."

True enough. On July 20, when Mother Margaret Mary glimpsed the beautiful little shrine which the novices had made, her eyes filled with happy tears.

"Children, the other Sisters simply must see what you've made!" she exclaimed joyfully. "Sister Frances Rosalie, Sister Péronne Margaret—perhaps you'd go and invite them?"

But even as the two were about to start happily on their way, Mother Margaret Mary had a sudden inspiration. First, she would kneel before the little shrine—the first altar in all the world to be dedicated to the Sacred Heart—and read an Act of Consecration which she had written. Then each of the novices could write a short Act of Consecration and read it aloud herself. After that, they would go to the cemetery to pray for the dead. When all these spiritual duties had been accomplished, then they would prepare to welcome their visitors to the novitiate.

So, considerably later in the day, Sister Frances Rosalie and Sister Péronne Margaret set out on their mission. However, very soon their youthful enthusiasm had begun to dwindle. Most of the older Sisters to whom they issued their invitations, including Sister Magdalen des Escures, had no interest in coming to see their new altar to the Sacred Heart.

"Your Mistress would do better to instruct you in the time-honored devotions of the Church," observed Sister Magdalen crisply.

"That's right," put in another well-meaning religious. "In former days the novices spent their time as novices should, in a devout study of the Holy Rule."

"Especially the part which reads: 'Let no one presume to introduce new prayers or offices, under any pretext whatsoever.'"

Visibly shaken, the two young messengers looked at each other in dismay. "Then...then you're not coming?" blurted out Sister Frances Rosalie, almost in tears.

"No, my dear, we're not," replied Sister Magdalen. "And you may explain to your Mistress, in detail, our very good reasons."

However, when they returned to the novitiate, the novices could not bear to tell the full story of what had happened. Several of their prospective guests could not come, explained Sister Frances Rosalie lamely, because they were...well...uh...

Tears filled Mother Margaret Mary's eyes as she sensed how her two young charges were trying to spare her feelings. "Never mind, little ones," she said hastily. "All this is God's Will, you know." Then, after a moment: "Perhaps some of the Sisters don't want to join us just now. But one of these days they'll be more than glad to honor the Sacred Heart of Jesus."

However, as the weeks passed, there seemed little hope that such a prophecy would be fulfilled. Indeed,

"THEY DON'T WANT TO COME AND SEE
THE SHRINE WE'VE MADE."

because of the storm of objections raised by certain important members of the community over the novices' altar to the Sacred Heart, Mother Melin soon found herself forced to issue some unpleasant orders. First, Mother Margaret Mary must confine all future mention of her cherished devotion to the novitiate. Second, for the time being she must stay away from Holy Communion on the First Fridays.

Mother Margaret Mary made no effort to argue her case, realizing the superior's line of reasoning only too well: that, for the present, the less prominence given to devotion to the Sacred Heart, the better. In God's own time the other Sisters might be given the grace to understand and embrace it. But now, when nerves were taut and the whole issue still under a cloud—

"My dear, you do understand, don't you?" asked Mother Melin anxiously. "I want to help you all I can, but the way things are...with so much criticism and unpleasantness...well, I scarcely know which way to turn."

Mother Margaret Mary nodded quietly. "Yes, Mother," she murmured. "I understand."

But when she was alone, a chill fear settled in Mother Margaret Mary's heart. Once, seven years before, Mother Greyfié had forbidden her to make the Holy Hour on Thursday nights. And with what disastrous results! Our Lord had been so displeased that almost immediately He had claimed the superior's beloved young friend, Sister Mary Elizabeth Quarré, as a victim of His justice. For no apparent reason she had had a violent hemorrhage, and had died quite suddenly in Mother Greyfié's arms.

"Oh, Lord, don't let anything like this happen again!" pleaded the Novice Mistress fearfully. "Mother Melin means no harm. She's only trying to help me—"

But even as she prayed, there was a rapid knocking at the door and Sister Marie Nicole, now the youngest of the novices, rushed frantically into the room. Her face was pale, her hands trembling.

"Mother, something terrible's happened!" she burst out. "Sister Frances Rosalie fainted a while ago...and now she's in dreadful pain...moaning and crying! And she doesn't seem to know any of us anymore, Mother! Or to want us to touch her! Oh, what are we going to do?"

Mother Margaret Mary stared in dismay. Not Sister Frances Rosalie, who had tried so hard to make her feast day memorable! Whom she loved as though she were her own child—

"Very well, Sister," she said quietly. "I'm coming."

CHAPTER 35

A STARTLING PROPHECY

SOON MOTHER Margaret Mary's worst fears were realized. Sister Frances Rosalie *was* ill, and of a complaint that completely baffled the community physician.

"I...I guess I'm going to die, Mother," she whimpered one morning, as the Novice Mistress bent over her bed. "And I'm so afraid...."

"No, no, dear," said Mother Margaret Mary hastily. "You're not going to die for a long time." Yet her heart was heavy as she gazed upon the young invalid. Why, the poor child was actually in agony! And to think that all this suffering might be connected in some way with Mother Melin's well-meant efforts to restore peace to the community....

"But what can I do?" she wondered painfully. "Our Lord *wants* me to obey my superior. He's told me that so often—"

However, as the days passed, Our Lord gave Mother Margaret Mary to understand that He was very displeased with Mother Melin. Until she permitted the resumption of the monthly Communions of reparation, Sister Frances Rosalie would continue to suffer.

Most reluctantly (for she had a horror of asking for

a favor once it had been taken from her), Mother Margaret Mary conveyed the news to her superior. But instead of being disturbed, Mother Melin was humility itself. She had displeased Our Lord? How dreadful! By all means Mother Margaret Mary must receive Holy Communion on the next First Friday, whether the other Sisters approved or not.

Wonders of wonders! Soon Sister Frances Rosalie had taken a turn for the better, and for the next three weeks the improvement continued. But as another First Friday approached, the Novice Mistress became prey to a sudden scruple. Hadn't the superior's permission been worded so as to include only the First Friday just passed, not every First Friday? If so, it surely wouldn't be right to approach the Holy Table again!

"Of course it would," said a prompting deep in her heart. "But if you like, explain things to Mother Melin. She'll understand."

However, Mother Margaret Mary could not bring herself to obey the prompting, with the result that she made no more Communions of reparation. Then presently Sister Frances Rosalie suffered a relapse. Indeed, when four months had passed, she was once again at death's door.

Beside herself with anxiety, the Novice Mistress finally sought out the Superior. For the sake of Sister Frances Rosalie, she asked humbly, wouldn't it be possible to receive Holy Communion on all the First Fridays, just as in the old days? So far Our Lord had been patient with the neglectful treatment meted out to Him. But soon, unless real reparation were made. . . .

Mother Melin turned pale. "Why, of course you may go to Holy Communion on all the First Fridays!" she burst out. "Oh, my dear, why didn't you ask me before about this foolish scruple?"

Mother Margaret Mary hung her head. "May God forgive my dreadful pride," she murmured contritely. "And you, too, Mother. . . ."

However, in just a short time there was reason for everyone to rejoice. Once again Sister Frances Rosalie was on the road to recovery.

"Mother, I don't think I'm going to die after all," she told the Novice Mistress one day. "Oh, how good God's been to me!"

Mother Margaret Mary smiled fondly at her young charge. "Yes, my dear, He has been good. You're going to live a long time, just as I told you in the first place. Besides—"

"What, Mother?"

"When I come to die, and that day isn't as far off as you may think, it will be in your arms."

This revelation was almost too much for the young novice. Mother Margaret Mary was actually intimating that her own death was not far away? Oh, no! Why, she was only thirty-eight years old! Yet soon the same startling prophecy was being made to another novice, Sister Péronne Rosalie. She, too, would support the Novice Mistress in her last agony.

Naturally Mother Melin was more than distressed to hear what Mother Margaret Mary had been saying. Why, as yet almost nothing had been done to promote a general devotion to the Sacred Heart! There was still a sizeable group in the monastery who didn't believe in Our Lord's apparitions. Even in town there were those who persisted in saying that the Novice Mistress was mentally ill and should never have been permitted to make her vows.

"Surely Mother Margaret Mary won't be leaving us

until all these misunderstandings have been cleared up," reflected the superior uneasily. "Or until something really definite has been done to promote devotion to the Sacred Heart. . . ."

Then shortly before Christmas, 1685, Mother Melin was given a new book, *Spiritual Retreat,* a collection of sermons preached by Father de la Colombière when he had been serving in London as private chaplain to the Duchess of York. And as she settled herself to leaf through the pages, she completely forgot her troubles. Why, here was an actual masterpiece on devotion to the Sacred Heart! Even more. There was frequent mention of "a person" whom God had chosen to enlighten the saintly Jesuit on what he should say and write—

"God having spoken to the person (who, we have reason to believe, is one after His own Heart, because He has given her great graces), she explained them to me, and I caused her to commit what she had told me to writing. . . .

"This person spoke thus: 'Being before the Blessed Sacrament one day during Its octave, I felt urged to make Him some return by giving Him back love for love. You cannot make Me any greater return for love, He said, than by doing what I have so often asked of you. Then, uncovering His Divine Heart, He said: Behold this Heart which has so loved mankind that It has spared Itself nothing, even to being spent and consumed to prove Its love for men. And yet It has received in return from the majority of mankind only ingratitude, coldness and the neglect of Me in the Sacrament of My love. But what is even more painful to Me is that it is hearts consecrated to Me which use Me thus. . . .'"

With trembling hands Mother Melin laid the book aside. Surely "the person" could be none other than Mother Margaret Mary!

"I'll have this book read in the refectory," she decided. "God willing, it may work a miracle where it's most needed."

CHAPTER 36

A GREAT CHANGE OF HEART

ALTHOUGH THE Rule prescribed that the Sisters maintain silence at meals, and keep their eyes lowered on their plates, there was a perceptible undercurrent of excitement when the name and author of the new choice for spiritual reading were announced. Why, this would be almost as though Father de la Colombière should come in person to speak to the community from his high place in Heaven!

But as the Sister reader commenced her task, a tense quiet began to settle over the refectory. Within minutes knives and forks were being laid aside, and there was no longer the slightest interest in food.

"...And so I ask you to have the Friday after the octave of Corpus Christi kept as a special Feast in honor of My Heart, by the receiving of Communion upon that day, and by making a reparation of honor for all the insults offered to the Host during Its exposition upon the altars...."

"Address yourself to My servant, and tell him from Me to do what he can to establish this devotion...."

The community sat at rigid attention. Then suddenly, the Rule forgotten, all eyes were on Mother Margaret Mary. Surely Father de la Colombière couldn't be referring to this humble religious, now covered with confusion, as the one that God had sent to help him in his great work! She who had been living among them for more than fourteen years—ridiculed, ignored, even persecuted—

"Oh, but it is!" thought Sister Frances Rosalie, happy tears glistening in her eyes. "It *is* our Mother!"

With difficulty the reader struggled on for several more minutes, trying to restrain an ever-increasing urge to look at Mother Margaret Mary, too. Then suddenly there were muffled sobs—first from one corner of the refectory, then from another. Quickly Mother Melin touched the small bell before her, an indication that the reading was sufficient for the present. And with a truly grateful heart, for seemingly Sister Magdalen des Escures had been among those most touched by the penetrating words of Father de la Colombière.

"Dear Lord, has it happened so soon?" she wondered in amazement. "Has there really been the miracle I was hoping for?"

The answer was not long in coming. During the recreation period which followed upon the main meal, Mother Margaret Mary found herself surrounded by the entire community. Some were weeping for joy. Others from remorse. Could the Novice Mistress ever forgive their blindness, their lack of charity, their failure to understand the beautiful devotion to which Father de la Colombière had dedicated the last years of his life?

"Oh, Mother, please, say you'll forgive and forget all my petty meanness!" burst out Sister Magdalen contritely. "I . . . I just haven't the words to tell you how sorry I am . . . ."

"And me, Mother!" put in Sister Antoinette de Coligny tearfully. "Can you ever forgive *me*?"

"SISTERS, THERE'S NOTHING TO FORGIVE!"

"And me?" blurted out a third religious. And a fourth. And a fifth.

Mother Margaret Mary scarcely knew where to turn. Suddenly the memory of the sufferings and misunderstandings of the past filled her heart with a surge of joy. These were the invincible weapons by which she had been able to make reparation for sinners. But now, surrounded by this admiring throng of fellow religious, sensing that all of them believed her to be a saint—

"Sisters, there's nothing to forgive!" she stammered. "I . . . I love you all! I always shall . . . ."

However, those who had so long opposed Mother Margaret Mary now realized their dreadful mistake, and nothing would do but that they try to make amends as quickly as possible. Thus, on the next First Friday, there was not one who did not receive Holy Communion. And of course Mother Melin was besieged by requests for a general Holy Hour every Thursday night. Even more. In January, 1686, when Mother Greyfié (now superior at Semur) sent the Novice Mistress a picture of the Sacred Heart which one of her Sisters had made, together with several smaller copies, there was great disappointment when it was found there were not enough of the latter to go around. After all, what was it Our Lord had said?

"I will bless the houses in which the image of My Sacred Heart shall be exposed and honored."

Well, if the monastery at Semur could have such pictures made and distributed, why couldn't the same be done at Paray-le-Monial? And certainly there ought to be a shrine in the chapel.

Mother Margaret Mary was beside herself with joy at this sudden change of heart. But it was on June 21, the Friday after the octave of Corpus Christi, that her happiness knew no bounds. Then Sister Magdalen des Escures announced that she had taken upon herself the erection of a shrine to the Sacred Heart in the convent chapel. It was only a temporary affair, of course, an effort to atone for her past pride and stubbornness, but perhaps Mother Margaret Mary would care to come and see it? And the other Sisters, too?

Sister Magdalen's shrine was a trifle crude, consisting merely of a chair set upon a piece of carpet before the iron grille, and on the chair a picture of the Sacred Heart, framed in gold, and surrounded by flowers. But the underlying thought touched Mother Margaret Mary deeply. Our Lord had been *enthroned!* He was King of the community! And on the very day which He had chosen for Himself eleven years before—the Feast of the Sacred Heart!

"How beautiful!" she exclaimed, almost in ecstasy. "Oh, Sister, how did you ever manage to think of anything like this?"

Such sincere praise from one who had every reason to be hurt, even resentful, over past injustices, was almost too much for Sister Magdalen. "It's nothing," she muttered gruffly. "What we really ought to have is an entire chapel dedicated to the Sacred Heart."

The Novice Mistress gasped. "A *chapel*, Sister! But where?"

"Oh, somewhere on the grounds. And don't worry about the expense, Mother. I'm sure we could raise the money in some way."

When she heard about the proposed plan, Mother Melin was enthusiastic. What a fine idea to have a chapel to the Sacred Heart! Of course the community was poor, but surely everyone would be able to interest friends and relatives in the project? And if the lay

Sisters would enlarge their vegetable and flower gardens, the additional revenue could be applied to it, too.

"If we all work together, I think we can afford to build a very nice chapel in two years' time," she said cheerfully.

So a drive for funds was begun, and by December of that same year a sizeable sum had been realized. But even as she rejoiced at such success, Mother Melin found herself faced with a problem. Attached to the monastery was a small school for girls, who, it was hoped, would someday develop true vocations to the Visitation Order. These girls ranged in age from ten to fifteen years, and their superior was known as the Mistress of Pupils. Unfortunately the present Mistress had not been well for some time, and soon it would be necessary to replace her. But with whom?

"Mother Margaret Mary would be ideal for the work," reflected the superior. "But then, who's to take her place in the novitiate? Why, the novices will be heartbroken if she has to leave them. . . ."

However, the more she thought about the matter, the more Mother Melin was convinced that Mother Margaret Mary ought to be the new Mistress of Pupils. Some thirteen years before she had held the office temporarily, and had done very well. Of course now there might be some who would think the position not sufficiently important for one who had been so greatly favored by Heaven. After all, what right had mere children to claim the full attention of a saint?

"But that's a terrible mistake to make," Mother Melin told herself. "Children are the hope of the future, the greatest treasure we have. As for the little ones living here at the monastery—well, the Visitation Order surely owes them the best training it can give."

So, early in 1687, Mother Melin calmly announced that she had appointed one of the older Sisters to take over the work in the novitiate. As for Mother Margaret Mary? Yes, she was the new Mistress of Pupils!

CHAPTER 37

SECRETS OF HOLINESS

NATURALLY the little girls in the monastery school were wildly excited at the news. Now they would be able to see Mother Margaret Mary every day, even several times a day. Perhaps she would work miracles, too—right before their eyes!

But one twelve-year-old, wiser than her companions, shook her head. "No, she didn't do that when she was here before, Sister Catherine says, and she won't do it now. She's not that kind of a saint."

At this there was general disappointment. "You mean she *can't* work miracles?"

"Of course she can. But she always works them when no one's looking. Like when she prayed in the chapel and cured her brother last month, although he was miles away."

This was news to several of the children. "What brother?" they chorused eagerly.

"Why, Father James Alacoque, the parish priest at Bois-Sainte-Marie. And now another brother is going to build a chapel to the Sacred Heart in thanksgiving."

"Another brother! What's his name?"

"I know!" put in a fourteen-year-old quickly. "It's Chrysostom Alacoque, the mayor of Bois-Sainte-Marie.

I saw him once when he came to visit Mother Margaret Mary."

The new Mistress of Pupils, chancing to pass by at the moment, smiled as she saw the earnest little group in such close conference in their recreation room. "Well, children, are you going over today's Catechism lesson?" she asked, a twinkle in her eye.

The twelve-year-old sighed blissfully. "No, Mother. We were just talking about. . .well, about a saint. And miracles."

"Saint Francis de Sales, dear, our holy Founder?"

"No, not Saint Francis."

"Then Mother de Chantal, who did so much to help him?"

"No, not Mother de Chantal either. Oh, Mother, we were talking about—"

But suddenly the Mistress of Pupils shook a warning finger. "No, don't tell me, children. Rather, let me ask you something. What *is* a saint?"

The little group looked at one another wide-eyed. Surely their Mistress, of all people, should know the answer to that question?

"Oh, Mother, a saint sees Our Lord all the time! And talks to Him, too!" exclaimed a ten-year-old eagerly.

"Yes. And a saint says a lot of long prayers every day and eats only a little bit of food," put in a solemn-faced companion.

For a moment the twelve-year-old was silent. Then she lifted glowing eyes to her superior. "That's right, Mother. But a saint does much more than *that!* He. . .she. . .works *miracles!* Like curing sick people. Or getting souls out of Purgatory when they deserve to stay there for years and years. Or. . .or maybe even raising the dead to life!"

Mother Margaret Mary smiled. "But I know several saints who wouldn't fit these descriptions," she protested mildly. "They don't see Our Lord, they eat three meals a day, and they've never worked a miracle in all their lives. What's more, Our Lord is very pleased with these good servants of His, and has the most wonderful reward waiting for them in Heaven."

The children stared in astonishment, particularly the fourteen-year-old. "But Mother, how can that be?" she burst out. "Why, I always thought—"

"Yes, dear, I know. You always thought a saint had to be—well, extreme. But there are many kinds of saints, and very often some of the greatest are men and women living ordinary lives in the world. Or boys and girls who haven't the slightest desire to be priests or brothers or nuns."

Silence fell over the group. There were saints in the world? Even children? Impossible!

As if she read their thoughts, Mother Margaret Mary began to explain, quite casually, that to be a saint one did not have to have visions or to work miracles. Why, even the Devil could see things hidden from earthly eyes! And work wonders, too, God not preventing him. Nor was it necessary that a saint should say long prayers, perform extreme mortifications or enter the priesthood or the religious life. No, all that was really needed for a person to be a saint was for him always to say "Yes" to God's Will. And what was God's Will in this seventeenth century, and in all the other centuries to come?

To love God very much—and our neighbor too. Ah, this was the key to holiness—and something the Devil could never do.

As Mother Margaret Mary continued, the children

were all attention. Yes, she sounded just like a saint. And she was telling *them* how to be saints, too!

"If you want to be a saint you must give Our Lord everything He asks you for," she warned the pupils kindly but firmly. "We cannot become saints by halves."

"And how do we know what He is asking of us?" the girls wanted to know.

"First, we are doing what God is asking when we obey our parents and teachers," answered Mother Margaret Mary. "But also, God often gives us the thought of doing some extra good deed—and when He does this, He also gives us the strength to carry it out. Don't refuse anything He asks of you. Great graces are often attached to what seems trifling and small."

Mother Margaret Mary explained many other things about being a saint, too. They certainly sounded like secrets of holiness!

On other occasions, the Mistress would tell the children, "You should never use your tongue to find fault with anyone but yourself, so that your tongue, on which the Sacred Host so often rests, may not be used by Satan to defile your soul." That was certainly something the pupils wanted to remember always.

Mother Margaret Mary also told the girls many things about suffering—things they would never have thought of by themselves. For instance, she explained that "In God's sight, our cross is like a precious perfume which loses its aroma when it is exposed to the air—so we must make every effort to hide our cross and carry it in silence."

Who would have thought that a little complaining could be so bad! Mother Margaret Mary went on to show the girls how their crosses were actually treasures that must not be lost.

MOTHER MARGARET MARY TOLD THEM
MANY SECRETS OF HOLINESS!

The Mistress of Pupils was always urging the girls—as she had urged the novices—to be perfectly faithful to Our Lord in everything, big or little.

And what did it mean to be faithful? It meant to do each task as well as possible—for Our Lord—even if no one was there to check it; to be kind to all the other girls, both to our favorites and those we don't feel particularly attracted to; to resist our little moods of laziness or irritability—making these little sacrifices for Our Lord. The Sacred Heart of Jesus would never refuse the strength and consolation needed, Mother Margaret Mary assured the pupils.

What confidence she gave them! Surely it would not be hard to become saints. But how did their Mistress know all these things? Why, she seemed to have learned them from Our Lord Himself!

Mother Margaret Mary also taught the children a special devotion of 33 Adorations of Jesus Crucified to perform silently in their hearts every Friday. It was a devotion to offer to the Heavenly Father for the conversion of hardened sinners. The girls were thrilled to have such a way to win graces of conversion for poor sinners who were headed for Hell.

Then there were two other special ways to love and honor Our Lord's Sacred Heart, Mother Margaret Mary explained to the children. Only the most serious reasons should ever keep them away from Holy Communion on the First Fridays and (if they were permitted) from making the Holy Hour on Thursday nights. To do these things was to give Our Lord some return for the blazing love of His Heart for us. Plus, it would make reparation for those who do not love Him—and also help to win back souls for Him. And although few people realized it just now, these two practices were so pleasing to God that He had arranged that those who followed them should become saints with amazingly little trouble.

Of course they would not necessarily *feel* holy. There would still be trials and temptations, perhaps even occasional lapses into sin. But little by little the transformation would come. For each time a person received Holy Communion worthily, God gave a share of His own perfection to that person—much or little, depending upon the care and love with which the Sacrament was received. Thus, in time that person could not help but become holier. He would begin to see things from God's own viewpoint, even crosses, and so enjoy a holy peace he had never experienced before.

"And when this happens, children, even to only one person, the whole Church benefits!" exclaimed the Mistress of Pupils, her eyes shining.

The ten-year-old nodded solemnly. "But surely many people could receive Our Lord on extra days like the First Fridays, Mother! And that would please Him, wouldn't it?"

"And make lots and lots of saints?"

A faint smile flickered on Mother Margaret Mary's lips. "That kind of reparation would turn this world into a little paradise," she murmured.

CHAPTER 38

THE GREAT PROMISE

DESPITE THE many hours she spent with the schoolgirls, the Mistress of Pupils was not unmindful of her many older friends—Mother Mary Frances de Saumaise, Mother Péronne Rosalie Greyfié, her own brothers Chrysostom and James, and several priests and religious throughout France who were doing what they could to spread devotion to the Sacred Heart. Indeed, the writing of letters to so many co-workers took up a great deal of time these days. But it was time well-spent, reflected Mother Margaret Mary, and those who received the letters agreed with her, especially Mother de Saumaise.

In fact, by March, 1688, Mother de Saumaise had only one worldly ambition, and that was to see Mother Margaret Mary once again. It was nearly ten years since she herself had left Paray-le-Monial for the Visitation monastery at Dijon, and so much had happened in the interval. How wonderful if the two of them could have just one good visit together!

But two months later this urge had become almost overpowering, especially when Mother de Saumaise received another letter from Mother Margaret Mary which set her pulse tingling. Apparently Our Lord had appeared once again in the chapel at Paray-le-Monial and had made a new promise—the twelfth—in favor of those who were devoted to His Sacred Heart. And what a glorious message He had brought this time!

"I promise you, in the excessive mercy of My Heart, that Its all-powerful love will grant to all those who communicate on the First Friday of every month for nine consecutive months the grace of final repentance. They shall not die in Its disfavor, nor without receiving their sacraments, and My Divine Heart will be their assured refuge at the last moment."

Mother de Saumaise could not take her eyes off the letter. Here, surely, was "The Great Promise" which Sister Anne Rosselin had hoped for so long ago, and many other people since. How Our Lord must love His creatures to give such a treasure for so little effort on their part!

However, some of the other Sisters were rather troubled by "The Great Promise." What did it mean, exactly? That a person who received Holy Communion on nine consecutive First Fridays could then become totally lax about his spiritual life, content that he would gain Heaven no matter what he did later on? Then, too, what was meant by that strange phrase, *"their* sacraments"? Could this possibly refer to the Last Sacraments of the Church? Certainly this was hard to believe, for undoubtedly there would be many good people in the years to come who, although they had made the nine First Fridays, would die without a priest.

For days Mother de Saumaise prayed and thought about the two problems, then presented her solution to the community. First, a person who received Communion with the intention of leading a bad life would be in the state of mortal sin—and of course Our Lord's promise applied only to *good* Communions, those received in the state of grace. Second, *"their* sacraments" did not necessarily mean the Last Rites of the Church: Confession, Holy Communion and Extreme Unction. Rather, the phrase referred to that state of soul known as "the state of grace."

"Then it all comes down to this," remarked one Sister thoughtfully. "Those who make the nine First Fridays and intend to lead good lives have God's own word that they'll have a happy death—with or without the Last Sacraments."

"Yes," said Mother de Saumaise. "That's exactly what 'The Great Promise' means—at least, in my opinion."

"Even though the death might be so sudden or tragic as to worry their friends and families?"

"That's right. God never goes back on His word."

Then presently one of the Sisters suggested a more troublesome problem. Suppose a person had made the nine First Fridays in good faith, then had drifted into a life of mortal sin and died in that state. Would he be saved by virtue of "The Great Promise"?

For a moment Mother de Saumaise was lost in thought, realizing that here was a question only an experienced theologian should decide. On the other hand, what about the passage in another letter from Mother Margaret Mary, written three years before, which she had been reading that very morning?

"He reassured me that the pleasure He has in being loved, known and honored by His creatures is so great that, if I be not mistaken, He promised that those who should be consecrated and devoted to Him should never be lost."

True, this passage did contain the somewhat misleading words, "if I be not mistaken." But, as most people knew nowadays, this was merely out of deference to a previous command of Mother Greyfié's that Mother Margaret Mary always preface any remarks about heavenly messages or visions with this or a similar expression.

"Sister," said Mother de Saumaise, looking earnestly at the last speaker, "if you want my opinion, here it is: any person who has made the nine First Fridays in good faith will never be lost."

The latter's eyes widened. "But Mother! It could be—"

"Yes, I know. It could be that the person might seem to have died in mortal sin. But God doesn't go back on His word, my dear. Somehow, in some way, He will surely grant that poor sinner the grace he needs—perhaps just before the soul leaves the body for judgment—to repent and return to His love."

There was such happy conviction in these words, such a warm sense of well-being and content, that Mother de Saumaise was even more astonished at what she had said than was her audience. Could she have spoken of herself, or had the Holy Spirit graciously spoken through her?

"It's...it's almost time for Vespers," she declared, visibly shaken. "That's enough talk for now, Sisters."

CHAPTER 39

A SPECIAL REQUEST

A MONTH LATER, even as Mother de Saumaise and her fellow-religious were still rejoicing over "The Great Promise," there came good news from England. On June 8, after years of anxious waiting on the part of the parents and the Catholic population of the country, another son had been born to King James the Second and Queen Mary Beatrice. And this time the royal infant was strong and healthy, giving every indication that he would live to manhood and some day ascend the English throne as King James the Third.

"God be praised!" was the cry that went up from thousands of grateful hearts. "Surely the prayers of Father de la Colombière have worked this wonder?"

The Jesuits in Paray-le-Monial were as pleased as everyone else at the news, and many were the acts of thanksgiving which they offered at the tomb of their deceased co-worker. But on July 2, the feast of the Visitation of the Blessed Virgin, there was even more cause for rejoicing. Then word came that Mother Margaret Mary had had another vision. This time she had seen Father de la Colombière in glory, together with Saint Francis de Sales, Our Lord, Our Lady and a host of the most exalted angels in Heaven—the Seraphim! And what a glorious message Our Lady had given her! Henceforth the Visitation Order would have the task of making devotion to the Sacred Heart known and loved throughout the world, assisted by the Fathers and Brothers of the Society of Jesus. In fact, the Jesuits would be so successful in this work that they could truly be likened to two-edged swords, able to penetrate the hearts of the most hardened of sinners.

As the days passed, the Sisters paid frequent visits to the little courtyard in the monastery where the latest vision had occurred, feeling sure that it was now a tremendously holy place. There were also many visits to the almost completed chapel of the Sacred Heart in the northeast corner of the garden. What a charming little sanctuary it was! And to think that everyone had had some part in making it possible! Even the children in the monastery school had generously contributed many pennies to the building fund.

Whenever Mother Melin visited the new chapel, she found it difficult to conceal her amazement. Why, it was only a little over a year since Sister Magdalen des Escures had first suggested such a project, and now there was more than enough money on hand to cover the entire building cost, as well as that of the furnishings!

"I think the dedication could take place early in September," she announced one day. "Everything should be ready by that time."

So at noon on September 7, 1688, all Paray-le-Monial proceeded to enjoy a general holiday. Benedictines, Jesuits, secular priests from far and near, went in procession to the Visitation monastery, followed by a devout crowd of the faithful. Hymns were sung, litanies

chanted, and then came the solemn ceremony of dedication. But when the three-hour service had ended,
there was considerable disappointment on the part of
several visitors. Where was Mother Margaret Mary?
Why wasn't she on the grounds with the other Sisters?
Or in the parlor?

The superior shook her head. Mother Margaret Mary
could see no one. She was...well, busy.

"But we came fifty miles to be here today!" protested
one woman. "Surely, if she knew that...."

"You see, our little John insists on asking her prayers,"
put in her husband anxiously, indicating his eight-year-
old son on crutches. "Poor lad, he's heard so much
about her, and has such wonderful faith—"

In spite of herself, Mother Melin was touched, especially at the sight of the little crippled boy. Ordinarily
the monastery garden, where the new chapel was situ-
ated, was closed to the public. But today, because of
the ceremony of dedication—

"Well, friends, come with me," she said kindly. "You
may not be able to speak with Mother Margaret Mary,
but at least you can see her."

So, with fast-beating hearts, the little group followed
the superior through the garden and into the recently
dedicated chapel. And there, far up the aisle, in a quiet
corner near the altar rail, knelt a solitary black-robed
figure.

"Didn't I tell you Mother Margaret Mary was busy?"
whispered Mother Melin. "She's been kneeling there
like that for several hours."

The visitors stared in awe. Here at last was the saint
of Paray-le-Monial! But what a disappointment not to
be able to have one word with her....

"There, now, you mustn't worry about that," said the

superior cheerfully when she had finally led the group back to the garden. "From past experience I know that Mother Margaret Mary realizes you're here, and why you've come, and that even now she's praying for all of you."

The little cripple looked up tearfully. "But she didn't even see us!" he protested. "She never even turned around...."

"Son, that doesn't matter in the least."

"B-but—"

"Just wait until you get home. Maybe there'll be a big surprise for you then, *if* you have faith."

However, when the visitors had finally taken their departure, Mother Melin returned to the back of the chapel in a troubled frame of mind. Had it been wise to suggest to that poor child and his parents that he might soon be cured? After all, who was to say what was God's Will for the young sufferer? But even as she dropped to her knees in a prayer for forgiveness, she looked up to see Mother Margaret Mary, her face radiant, standing beside her.

"It's all right, Mother," whispered the latter softly.

When the two nuns had stepped outside the chapel, Mother Margaret Mary explained: "Our Lord is very pleased with those good people for coming here today to honor His Sacred Heart. He plans to cure the boy when they get home, just as you hoped."

The superior drew back in amazement. "But they never mentioned the Sacred Heart, Mother! It seemed that it was really you they came to see...."

Mother Margaret Mary smiled. "For a long time now that little lad has been very dear to Our Lord," she said quietly. "In his own simple way he's been trying to honor the Sacred Heart, even to offering his sufferings in reparation for sinners."

"In reparation for sinners! But how could a mere child know about that?"

"Because his parents have been reading one of those wonderful little pamphlets on devotion to the Sacred Heart, Mother. The boy listened, grasped what he could, and the Holy Spirit did the rest."

Slowly the superior rose to her feet. There was no use in hoping that Mother Margaret Mary would admit to having helped the visitors by her prayers. Or in pointing out that even her knowledge of their presence and of the details of their problem, and the promised solution, were in themselves beyond human power. No, as in the past, when such things had happened, it was best to let the whole matter drop.

But the pamphlet on the Sacred Heart which had been prepared in Moulins two years before by their mutual friend, Mother de Soudeilles? Ah, that was something different. Sometime soon they must have a good talk about that.

CHAPTER 40

PRECIOUS LAST DAYS

MOTHER MARGARET Mary was only too pleased to talk about the pamphlet, also about an even more complete explanation of the Sacred Heart devotion which was being prepared in the Visitation monastery at Dijon. If all went well, several hundred copies of this new book would be available early in 1689. And what wonderful good it would accomplish! Why, with the cooperation of Mother de Saumaise, Mother Greyfié, Mother de Soudeilles and various Jesuit priests and brothers, there was every reason to believe that very soon the need for devotion to the Sacred Heart would be known throughout the whole country!

However, shortly before the book's appearance, there came a crushing blow for Catholics everywhere. On November 5, 1688, ran the report, the armies of Prince William of Orange had landed in England. Backed by disgruntled Protestant leaders there, the invaders had forced King James the Second to vacate his throne and finally to flee to France with his wife and six-month-old son. Now Parliament had declared William to be the lawful ruler of the land, together with his wife, the former Princess Mary.

"But that's not right!" protested honest statesmen everywhere. "King James is a good Christian man, with the interests of his country much at heart. As for Queen Mary Beatrice—why, she's practically a saint!"

"Yes, but they're both Catholics," was the answer. "And seemingly the Devil feels they're spoiling his plan to ruin the cause of the Church in England—especially now that they have a healthy son and heir."

"You mean that the little Prince will never reign as King James the Third?"

"Not if the Devil can help it."

Soon this dire prophecy was being realized. Indeed, by the spring of 1690 it was openly conceded that if William and Mary died childless, the throne would go to Mary's younger sister Princess Anne, now the wife of Prince George of Denmark. And if these two should leave no children—well, some distant Protestant relative, possibly one living in Germany, would have to be brought over to rule.

At Saint-Germain-en-Laye, their new home near Paris, the royal exiles heard these rumors with a heavy heart. How hard they had tried to serve their country! And how happy they had been when Heaven had sent them a little son who one day would have been able to carry on the work in their place! But now—

"We really shouldn't complain, though, James," the thirty-two-year-old Queen reminded her husband one day. "After all, this trial comes from God. Surely we ought to accept it as such, especially in a spirit of reparation to the Sacred Heart?"

The King, looking far older than his fifty-seven years, managed a faint smile. "Yes," he said heavily. "I suppose that's what Father de la Colombière would want us to do."

And so, as best they could, the royal couple set themselves to bear their heavy cross more cheerfully. Some day, God willing, their sacrifice would produce rich fruit for the Mystical Body of Christ. The English people would recognize the error of their ways and return to the True Church. Possibly even the reigning sovereign would be among them.

Meanwhile, in Paray-le-Monial, one hundred and eighty miles to the southeast of Paris, there was astonishment over the fact that on July 22, her forty-third birthday, Mother Margaret Mary had begun a forty-day retreat in preparation for her death. Her work on earth was about finished, she insisted, and she would die before the end of the year.

The new superior, Mother Catherine Antoinette de Lévy-Châteaumorand (who had succeeded Mother Melin in May), scarcely knew what to say. How could Mother Margaret Mary think her earthly work was finished when there was still so much to be done to promote devotion to the Sacred Heart? To explain the true meaning of a Communion of reparation on the First Fridays and the Holy Hour on Thursday nights?

Then one day, late in September, the community physician, Doctor William Billet, had most encouraging news. "I think our good saint has made a mistake this time," he told the superior cheerfully. "She's really going to be with us for many years. In fact, that long retreat must have been just what she needed, for she's more rested and in far better health than when she began to make it."

Happy tears filled the eyes of Mother Catherine Antoinette. "Thank God!" she exclaimed. "I just don't know what we'd do without her, Doctor."

However, Mother Margaret Mary continued to insist

that soon God would be calling her home. And on the morning of October 16, feeling strangely weak and faint, she humbly asked permission to receive the Last Rites of the Church.

"Now, my dear, there's no need for that," said Mother Catherine Antoinette kindly. "You're just a bit overtired, that's all. A day or two in bed, and you'll be quite yourself again."

The invalid's lips trembled. "No, Mother. I'm going to die. Oh, surely you'll let me receive Holy Communion this morning? It...it will be for the last time...."

In spite of herself, a sudden pang of anxiety shot through the superior's heart. Could Doctor Billet have made a mistake? Was Mother Margaret Mary really gravely ill?

"Of course you may receive Holy Communion," she said, her eyes troubled. "And if there's anything else you want—"

But Mother Margaret Mary shook her head. "No, Mother. That's all," she whispered.

However, a new request did come from the sickroom towards evening, which Mother Catherine Antoinette hastened to grant. Yes, Sister Marie Nicole, a former novice of the patient's, might sit up with her. (Mother Margaret Mary said she wanted to have Sister Marie Nicole by her when she died!) And there was no need for the younger religious to be fearful. Sister Catherine Marest, the ever-faithful infirmarian, would be only a few steps away if anything should go wrong.

As darkness settled over the monastery, Sister Marie Nicole took up her place by Mother Margaret Mary's bed. A single oil lamp cast eerie shadows on the wall. All was silent, and for a moment the newcomer felt that merciful sleep must have come to her charge. How still she lay, a peaceful smile upon her lips, a crucifix within her limp hands! But suddenly Mother Margaret Mary stirred and opened her eyes.

"Little Aloysius Gonzaga," she whispered faintly, "come closer, dear. There's something I want to say to you."

The pet name from her novitiate days (when she had been the youngest in the class) awakened a flood of grateful memories in the heart of Sister Marie Nicole. What a good friend the Novice Mistress had been during those dreadful weeks of homesickness when she had both feared and doubted her vocation!

"Yes, Mother? You wanted something?"

"Ah, child, indeed I do! Promise to make the Sacred Heart known and loved. . .to tell people about the First Fridays. . .the Communion of reparation. . .the Holy Hour. . . ."

"But Mother—"

"Mark my words well, little one. Someday you will be the superior here, with power to do much good for souls."

Sister Marie Nicole turned pale. She, the superior at Paray-le-Monial? Oh, no! But even as she attempted to protest, Mother Margaret Mary stretched out her hand.

"Listen, little Aloysius Gonzaga. The world is a cold and lonely place without the love of God and neighbor in one's heart. And yet both are to be had so easily, almost for the asking. . . ."

Sister Marie Nicole swallowed hard. "You mean—?"

"Holy Communion is the secret, especially the Holy Communion of reparation on the First Fridays. Oh, if I could just make everyone understand how Our Lord *wants* to live in their hearts! And the wonderful blessings He has for those friends who invite Him. . ."

CHAPTER 41

THE DEATH OF A SAINT

EARLY THE next morning, when Mother Catherine Antoinette came to the sickroom, she found Sister Marie Nicole in a state bordering upon ecstasy. What wonderful things Mother Margaret Mary had been telling her during the night, especially concerning those men, women and children who were not afraid to make reparation for sinners! Who were wise enough, after they had received Holy Communion, to beg God to let them know and love Him more and more each day so that they might better carry His message to friends and neighbors!

Then there was also the startling prophecy about their own little town of Paray-le-Monial—

"Our monastery is going to be famous, Mother!" whispered Sister Marie Nicole excitedly. "It's going to be the center for worldwide devotion to the Sacred Heart! Tonight is the beginning."

Mother Catherine Antoinette stared in amazement. *"Tonight,* Sister?"

"Yes. Mother Margaret Mary is going to Heaven then. And after her death, thousands of people will be coming here to learn about the First Fridays."

The superior shrugged, then moved briskly toward

the bed. What child's talk was this? But as she gazed down upon the invalid, her face suddenly turned pale. Why, Mother Margaret Mary was scarcely breathing! And her eyes were clouded with pain. . . .

"Quick, call Sister Catherine!" she ordered. "And send for Doctor Billet, too!"

Soon word was going about the monastery that Mother Margaret Mary had taken a sudden turn for the worse. A violent fever had come upon her, and she was in great agony. Amazed and fearful, the Sisters hurried to the sickroom, or knelt in anxious little groups in the corridor outside. Why, only a few hours before the doctor had said that Mother Margaret Mary was in no danger! But now—

"She *is* dying!" burst out Sister Frances Rosalie tearfully. "I know it!"

However, many in the community could not bring themselves to believe the dreadful news. Mother Margaret Mary was a comparatively young woman, only forty-three years old. Surely God would hear their prayers and leave her with them to do more work for souls? But as the hours passed, the experienced infirmarian, Sister Catherine Marest, realized the truth. It would soon be time for Mother Margaret Mary to receive the Last Sacraments.

Towards seven o'clock in the evening, everything being in readiness, the convent chaplain arrived for the last anointing. The little room was crowded with weeping religious, but Sister Marie Nicole remained composed. How could she be sad, after listening to Mother Margaret Mary? "Ah, what happiness it is to love God!" the dying nun had exclaimed. "Let us love Him! Let us love Him! But let us love Him *perfectly!*"

How great was Mother Margaret Mary's desire to see

THEY BENT FORWARD TO SUPPORT THEIR
FORMER NOVICE MISTRESS WITH LOVING CARE.

God in Heaven! "Soon her hope will be fulfilled," thought Sister Marie Nicole. "This will be the happiest moment of her life—the entrance to eternal joy, the only birthday that matters!"

Now the priest was saying the prayers for the dying. "*...May the heavens be opened to her, may the angels rejoice with her. Receive Thy handmaid, O Lord, into Thy kingdom. Let Saint Michael, the Archangel of God, who is the chief of the heavenly host, conduct her. Let the holy angels of God come forth to meet her, and carry her to the city of the heavenly Jerusalem....*"

On either side of the bed, just as Mother Margaret Mary had foretold long ago, Sister Frances Rosalie and Sister Péronne Rosalie bent forward to support their former Novice Mistress with loving care.

Slowly Mother Margaret Mary closed her eyes, her face beautiful beyond words in the light of the flickering candles. Then she smiled, like a tired child ready for sleep.

"Jesus," she whispered softly. And bowed her head.

St. Meinrad, Indiana
Feast of the Immaculate Heart of Mary
August 22, 1953

HISTORICAL NOTE

Margaret Mary Alacoque was declared Venerable on March 30, 1824. She was beatified on September 18, 1864, and canonized on May 13, 1920.

Father Claude de la Colombière was declared Venerable on January 8, 1880, and accorded the honors of beatification on June 16, 1929. He was canonized on May 31, 1992.

The Feast of the Sacred Heart was extended to the Universal Church on August 23, 1856.

Also by the same author . . .

6 <u>MORE</u> GREAT CATHOLIC BOOKS FOR CHILDREN
. . . and for all young people ages 10 to 100!!

1200 SAINT THOMAS AQUINAS—The Story of "The Dumb Ox." 81 pp. PB. 16 Illus. Impr. The remarkable story of how St. Thomas, called in school "The Dumb Ox," became the greatest Catholic teacher ever.   6.00

1201 SAINT CATHERINE OF SIENA—The Story of the Girl Who Saw Saints in the Sky. 65 pp. PB. 13 Illus. The amazing life of the most famous Catherine in the history of the Church.   5.00

1202 SAINT HYACINTH OF POLAND—The Story of The Apostle of the North. 189 pp. PB. 16 Illus. Impr. Shows how the holy Catholic Faith came to Poland, Lithuania, Prussia, Scandinavia and Russia.   11.00

1203 SAINT MARTIN DE PORRES—The Story of The Little Doctor of Lima, Peru. 122 pp. PB. 16 Illus. Impr. The incredible life and miracles of this black boy who became a great saint.   7.00

1204 SAINT ROSE OF LIMA—The Story of The First Canonized Saint of the Americas. 132 pp. PB. 13 Illus. Impr. The remarkable life of the little Rose of South America.   8.00

1205 PAULINE JARICOT—Foundress of the Living Rosary and The Society for the Propagation of the Faith. 244 pp. PB. 21 Illus. Impr. The story of a rich young girl and her many spiritual adventures.   13.00

1206 ALL 6 BOOKS ABOVE (Reg. 50.00)   THE SET: 40.00

Prices guaranteed through December 31, 1998.

U.S. & CAN. POST./HDLG.: $1-$10, add $2; $10.01-$20, add $3; $20.01-$30, add $4; $30.01-$50, add $5; $50.01-$75, add $6; $75.01-up, add $7.

**At your Bookdealer or direct from the Publisher.
Call Toll Free 1-800-437-5876**

More books by the same author . . .

<u>8 MORE</u> GREAT CATHOLIC BOOKS FOR CHILDREN

. . . and for all young people ages 10 to 100!!

1230 SAINT PAUL THE APOSTLE—The Story of the Apostle to the Gentiles. 231 pp. PB. 23 Illus. Impr. The many adventures that met St. Paul in the early Catholic Church.　　　　13.00

1231 SAINT BENEDICT—The Story of the Father of the Western Monks. 158 pp. PB. 19 Illus. Impr. The life and great miracles of the man who planted monastic life in Europe.　　　　8.00

1232 SAINT MARGARET MARY—And the Promises of the Sacred Heart of Jesus. 224 pp. PB. 21 Illus. Impr. The wonderful story of remarkable gifts from Heaven. Includes St. Claude de la Colombière.　　　　11.00

1233 SAINT DOMINIC—Preacher of the Rosary and Founder of the Dominican Order. 156 pp. PB. 19 Illus. Impr. The miracles, trials and travels of one of the Church's most famous saints.　　　　8.00

Continued on next page . . .

**At your Bookdealer or direct from the Publisher.
Call Toll Free 1-800-437-5876**

1234 KING DAVID AND HIS SONGS—A Story of the Psalms. 138 pp. PB. 23 Illus. Impr. The story of the shepherd boy who became a warrior, a hero, a fugitive, a king, and more.
8.00

1235 SAINT FRANCIS SOLANO—Wonder-Worker of the New World and Apostle of Argentina and Peru. 205 pp. PB. 19 Illus. Impr. The story of St. Francis' remarkable deeds in Spain and South America.
11.00

1236 SAINT JOHN MASIAS—Marvelous Dominican Gatekeeper of Lima, Peru. 156 pp. PB. 14 Illus. Impr. The humble brother who fought the devil and freed a million souls from Purgatory.
8.00

1237 BLESSED MARIE OF NEW FRANCE—The Story of the First Missionary Sisters in Canada. 152 pp. PB. 18 Illus. Impr. The story of a wife, mother and nun—and her many adventures in pioneer Canada.
9.00

1238 ALL 8 BOOKS ABOVE (Reg. 76.00) THE SET: 60.00

Prices guaranteed through December 31, 1998.

Get the Complete Set!! . . .

SET OF ALL 20 TITLES

by Mary Fabyan Windeatt

(Individually priced—179.00   Reg. set prices—143.00)

1256 THE SET OF ALL 20 . . . . Only 125.00

U.S. & CAN. POST./HDLG.: $1-$10, add $2; $10.01-$20, add $3; $20.01-$30, add $4; $30.01-$50, add $5; $50.01-$75, add $6; $75.01-up, add $7.

**At your Bookdealer or direct from the Publisher.
Call Toll Free 1-800-437-5876**

TAN BOOKS AND PUBLISHERS, INC.
P.O. Box 424
Rockford, Illinois 61105